MW00354338

FINALLY FREE

FINALLY FREE

DR. NICOLE SCOTT

Palmetto Publishing Group
Charleston, SC

Finally Free
Copyright © 2020 by Dr. Nicole Scott
All rights reserved

No portion of this book may be reproduced, stored in a retrieval system, or transmitted in any form by any means–electronic, mechanical, photocopy, recording, or other except for brief quotations in printed reviews, without prior permission of the author.

First Edition

Printed in the United States

ISBN-13: 978-1-64111-900-9
ISBN-10: 1-64111-900-4

TABLE OF CONTENTS

FOREWORD

I am delighted to write this foreword, not only because Nicole Scott is my best friend and a colleague but more importantly, she is my daughter. As a social worker and educator, I was absolutely enthralled by the raw honesty she displayed in telling her story. She was able to stand in her truth to display vulnerability and share mistakes and triumphs she had in her journey of life. This memoir is raw and honest. Nicole did not provide you the opportunity to *peek* into her life—she opened wide her entire house to the reader to *witness* her journey through years of hurt, pain, and growth. She is an accomplished individual: she earned her master's degree in her early twenties and secured her doctorate degree before she was thirty-four years of age. She is focused, driven, and awe-inspiring.

Nicole is a social worker, educator, and, through this book, a counselor. She authored a book that speaks to your heart and will have you reflecting, wow, we all have the same life experiences, no matter our ages or socioeconomic statuses. From the time Nicole was a little girl, she was a charismatic, thoughtful, and caring individual. When she spoke, you listened because you knew she was going to say something thought provoking. As she grew into a fine young woman, she developed a wicked sense of humor and maintained her tender heart.

As her mother who witnessed her journey, I believe deeply in the educative value of her captivating memoir. She provides insight and offers the "why" and then provides strategies on how you can *finally be free*! I hope this book becomes a guide for all individuals to live their best life.

Lenore Scott

INTRODUCTION

When people would look at me, they would think that I had *everything* together. I grew up in a two-parent household in a middle-class neighborhood with more than enough resources at my disposal, so some may think that I was spoiled by my parents. Both of my parents are college educated and have/had great careers. My father was a nuclear chemist before retiring, and my mom works in social work administration. My father was and still is a pillar of the community in which I grew up, and my mom is in the social work field and has always had the passion to help others. As a result, it was only natural that I would follow in their footsteps. I went to Florida State University for undergrad on an athletic scholarship, I purchased my first home before the age of thirty, and I earned my doctoral degree by the age of thirty-three. I share the same passion of helping others (especially children) as my parents. I served on many nonprofit boards, and I am big on community service. Despite all of these accomplishments, I still found myself in a position where I was ready to give up on myself. And despite all of the people who love me and care about me, I did not love myself. What do you do when you are considered the strong one and you no longer have the fight to go on? This memoir is going to talk about how one can find themselves in the darkest of spaces when they do not love themselves. And the craziest part of all of this is that my life did not begin to truly unravel until the age of thirty-seven.

This book will share the good, the bad, and the ugly...But most importantly, this book will share my journey, my spiritual awakening, and the road to self-awareness, self-love, and self-worth. I want this book to encourage someone who may feel hopeless, feel like throwing in the towel, or just want to give up and end it all. But by the grace of God I am still here. When one begins to be introspective and do the work necessary to get to know themselves, there is nothing but greatness on the other side. I wrote this book in hopes of being an inspiration to you by letting you know that we all fall short in life sometimes, but that does not mean that is where we will stay. And although as you are going through a storm you may not see the light at the end of the tunnel, I am a living testimony that trouble doesn't last forever. This book will share my struggle as well as tips, strategies, and activities that helped me along the way that I hope will also help you as well. Here is my story.

CHAPTER 1

Suffering in Silence

Sometimes the strongest among us are the ones who smile through the silent pain, cry behind closed doors, and fight battles nobody knows about.
—Unknown

What do you do when your life has crumbled before you and everything you once knew is no more? I found myself in a space where I felt alone, lost, and losing my will to live. I had an unexplainable void in my life, and the only solution I thought was left was to just not have to feel the pain and hurt anymore. In my mind and heart, life just wasn't worth living anymore. I had a hole in my heart, and no one could fill that void. I had an emptiness in my soul that no one could understand, so I chose to suffer in silence.

Let me take you to January 5, 2017, when my life changed forever. I was a mom for eight years of my life. My daughter came into my life back in 2009 at the age of one from a previous relationship. I loved her just like she was my own. When I purchased my house in September 2009, her and her father moved in with me. From that moment on, I dedicated my life to being the best mother I could be, especially because her biological mother wasn't in her life. She called me Mommy, and I was the only mother she knew because she came into my life as a baby.

Anyone who knows me knows that I love kids, and I was so grateful to have the opportunity to experience motherhood. We did everything together, and my family accepted her as well. My parents were Mom-Mom and Pop-Pop, and my brothers were her uncles. We traveled together, and she even joined the same dance school I did as a child. She was involved in Girl Scouts just like me as well. I wanted her to be exposed to as many things as possible. I had an amazing childhood, and I wanted to provide that to her. We went to church together with my mom, and she was in the Bible study club at her school as well as on the track team. I was very involved in her schooling, and all the staff knew who I was. She was a girly-girl just like me. We were joined at the hip.

Well, on the night of my birthday celebration, which was January 4, 2017, my life as I knew it (or so I thought) was over. Because my daughter's phone was connected to mine, my Gmail account was on her phone. Her father was going through her phone and saw some email exchanges between myself and an attorney. I was simply wanting some guidance on how I could establish some legal rights for myself when it came to my daughter. It made sense to me since she was living with me full time. At the time, our relationship was not the best, so every time he would get upset with me, he would take her away from me. There would be times he would say I couldn't see her anymore, and she would be gone for a week or two. I just wanted to eliminate all of that back and forth.

The next morning I gave her a kiss and put her on the bus, not knowing that would be the last time I would see or talk to her for seven months. I did not see her again until August 2017. There was no goodbye, no closure, nothing. And this was when my life began to take a downward spiral. Up until this point, she had lived with me, gone to school in the town where I own my home, and being as though I have a background in education, I was beyond involved in her schooling from day one.

Once she was taken away from me, I did not know what to do with myself. At first, I thought this was going to be just like all the other times and I would be hearing from her soon, but as weeks passed, I knew this time was different. I spent day after day suffering in silence. I had to live two lives at this point. One where I had to pretend everything was OK, especially at work. I would try to conduct business as usual at work. And when the pain became too much to bear, I would sit in my car and sob uncontrollably. The saddest part of it all is that my parents and my older brother lived about five minutes from my job. But I never went over there. I felt like no one would understand my pain because, to the average person, they did not understand. I even had friends be insensitive enough to say that maybe this was God telling me that it was time to let go. I would *never* say this to anyone. Because to me she was my daughter. Would they say that to someone if that was their biological child? It was at that point that I realized I should keep my pain to myself. Except for those truly close to me, I never disclosed what was going on in my life. There were days that I could not get out of bed. There were times that my phone would ring and I would just stare at it but refuse to answer. There were times that one of my neighbors would knock on my door to check on me and I would act like I wasn't home. Day after day I would go through life, either numb, completely broken, or contemplating, "Why even be here anymore?"

Not a day would go by without me wondering if she was OK. I would ask myself: Was she thinking about me? Was she crying or sad? Did she think I abandoned her or walked away from her? These questions ran through my head daily because I never wanted her to think that she wasn't wanted or loved. Unfortunately, there was no way for me to let her know that. Looking at her pictures hanging around the house became too much to bear. Every time I would look at one of her pictures, I would break down and cry. Every time I found a note lying around the house saying things such as "Mommy, I love you so much," I would lose it. It was so bad that I even kept the door to her bedroom closed because I could not stand to see her empty room day after day. I made sure to leave her room just like it was when she left because, despite all the pain, I kept a mustard seed of faith and kept telling myself that she would be back home soon.

When her birthday came around in June, that was the lowest point for me. I hadn't missed a birthday since she was two years old, and here I was missing her tenth birthday. Her first year in the double digits, and I couldn't be there to make a big deal about being in the double digits. Not being able to sing happy birthday to her or see her was beyond devastating. That was the day that I wished I couldn't feel pain anymore. I was ready to die.

It is so funny, but support always comes from the places you least expect it. There was a staff member at her school who always took a liking to my daughter. From day one, I asked her if she would look out for my daughter. Over 90 percent of the staff at her school was white. There were only two black people in the school, and this staff member was one of them. So naturally my daughter gravitated to her. She took my daughter under her wing, and that meant the world to me. Once I finally mustered up the strength to tell her what happened, she did not hesitate to jump right in, and she became my prayer warrior. She would send me text messages with scriptures attached, she would send me pictures of her from activities that went on at the school, and she would just encourage me to press on day after day. She would check in often to find out the status of the court case. She is truly a godsend, and I will forever be grateful for her. We continue to stay in touch to this day, and we try to meet when our schedules permit for breakfast or brunch.

I had been seeing my therapist for years now at this point, and she has helped me through many other trials and tribulations. But never did I think that I would be sitting in front of her broken to pieces and not feeling like I could go on. The craziest part is therapy is where I am supposed to be my most vulnerable self, and I could not even do it. I could not even utter the words to my therapist that I no longer had the will to live. I was scared for several reasons because I knew this would mean her having to report my thoughts of suicide, and I did not want to be committed to an institution. I was embarrassed that someone who was so strong had finally lost her will to fight. There was a little piece of me that thought, What if by some strange chance she would come back into my life, but I had chosen to end my life? How would that make my daughter feel?

Although I never had any actual suicide attempts, I often thought about not having to feel this pain anymore. And I often thought that the only way to not feel this pain was to end it all. But despite all of the hurt, pain, and anger, something in the back of my mind kept telling me to just hold on and fight.

One day I woke up, and I felt different. Although I was still hurting, I had the strange urge to get up and do something about this situation. I no longer wanted my pain to win. I wanted my pain to fuel my fight to get my baby back. I got up that morning, and I started researching family law attorneys. Now I knew I was up for a fight, but I had no idea I was in for the fight of my life.

I spoke to several attorneys. I even reached out to my good friend Trinetta who is an attorney in Florida for advice. Some consultations were free, and some came at a hefty price. The end result was that many of them did not want to take my case because of the fact that it wasn't an easy one to win. The last meeting my father attended with me and the lawyer wanted a $6,000 retainer. At the time, I was not financially prepared for that. At that moment, I was going to give up, but then my father reminded me as we were walking out that us Scotts don't quit. So once I got home, I started doing some more research, and I found the perfect attorney. My mother and I attended the initial consultation, and it ended up being a great consultation, and although he let me know that this would not be an easy thing to prove, he was certainly up for the challenge.

What the attorney educated my mother and me on was the term *psychological parent*. A psychological parent is someone who is not blood or an adoptive *parent* to a child but third parties that fit very specific standards set by the court. In order for the court to deem me as a psychological parent, I had to meet four specific criteria, which were: the biological parent consents to and fosters the person's formation of a parent-like relationship with the child, living in the same household for a certain period of time, assuming obligation of parenthood, and having a bonded and dependent relationship. I knew that I met all four criteria, I just needed to make sure that I had the evidence to substantiate it. Finally, I got the little glimmer of hope that I was praying for. And that night I put my armor on and prepared for the fight of my life.

Although my attorney told me that this would not be easy and had the likelihood to be a long process, there was still part of me that felt like I would go to court one time, the judge would see all of my evidence, and my daughter would be back. Boy, was I wrong! Month after month I would hit roadblock after roadblock. My faith had never been tested to this magnitude. Ever! Despite everyone telling me to stay strong and keep the faith, all it did was make me more upset. It is always so easy to tell someone what to do when they are not going through it.

It still was an unexplainable pain that I felt every day. All the while, I had to keep a facade at work when people would ask me about her. When kids in the neighborhood would ask where she was and I would lie and say I put her in private school, when my neighbors would ask where she was, it became too much to bear. I cried out to my therapist one day about having to keep up this facade. How I was drained from almost having to live two separate lives. One that was filled with such loss, despair, and sorrow. And another life that presented itself as normal and happy. She explained that with all I was going through in this season, trying to keep up appearances was the least of my worries. At the end of the day, I owed no one anything. Not a lie, not an excuse, not even a justification. The only person I owed something to was myself. I owed myself the right to just be.

All my life I was always concerned about everyone else but me. I was always worrying about what someone would think or say. And this caused me to be in this very predicament. So that session with my therapist freed me in a sense. It gave me permission to break free. To break free from all the guilt, hurt, shame, and embarrassment that I had been feeling. The next day I told a few people that were close to me what was going on (outside of the people that already knew). And after that, I felt better. And where I thought that they were going to judge me, they actually responded better than some of those closest to me, including a so-called boyfriend who told me that it was time for me to give this whole thing up (but I will get more into him in the next chapter). This awakening was the small ounce of relief that I experienced during this whole ordeal.

Month after month I felt like I wasn't getting any closer to a resolution. Anything that could've went wrong did, from the first court date getting a continuance because her father's lawyer just got the petition and needed more time to review, to then him switching counsel and then that attorney needing more time to review and then getting another continuance, to my attorney not showing up to a court appearance and the judge completely going apeshit because of it. All of my family was there that day, and we were sent home. It was after that court date that I broke down in tears because I was thinking that this was going to count negatively against me. I kept saying, "Why does this keep happening to me?" This wasn't a divorce that was trying to get mediated. This was a child. And every day that went by, every continuance that was granted, it was another day that my heart ached, another day that I did not get to see her, another day that I wondered if she was OK. I could not see the light at the end of the tunnel.

Finally, after six months of back and forth, the day finally came. The judge was ready to hear my case. And I was more than ready. My parents, my sister-in-law as well as my best friend,

Angel, whom I call my sister, a former coworker/friend, and my boyfriend at the time were there with me. This turned out to be one of the longest days ever. We went all day with only a short break. I had a major migraine from all of the stress, anticipation, hope, and confusion. The day started with Angel testifying, then my former coworker/friend, my boyfriend, my father, and then my mom. Each time someone new got on the stand, I could feel my stress levels increasing. I kept saying to myself, "I hope no one loses their cool, I hope no one says the wrong thing, I hope my daughter's dad doesn't anger anyone (especially my father) to the point of no return." My sis Angel did an amazing job. I was so glad that we started the court proceedings off with her. Angel loved my daughter. My daughter called her auntie Angel and my daughter called Angel's daughter "sis." Angel knew first hand the bond I had with my daughter because we were always spending time together with our daughters. There was a lot at stake for Angel as well because her daughter missed spending time with my daughter. Angel was due to be out of town for a work trip the day of my hearing but she told her boss that this court appearance was something she could not miss. She literally bolted out the door after testifying. I am so thankful for Angel.

We made it up through lunchtime, and all my witnesses had taken the stand except for my mom. None of the witnesses were allowed in the room when anyone else was testifying, so everyone was in the waiting area on pins and needles. It was just me, my attorney, her dad, and the judge. I felt like everything was going well for the most part, but I was still a nervous wreck because I knew after recess, I would also have to take the stand. It was so much easier when I could blame it on someone else for losing their cool or saying the wrong thing, but what about me? I had waited six long months for this day, but little did I know I would be a ball of nerves when the day finally came. I kept saying to myself that everything was going to be OK. And along the way after each person got a chance to testify, the judge would ask if her dad wanted to mediate, and he would decline. The judge kept saying that once he ruled, the ruling would be final, so he wanted to give her dad a chance to mediate. I got the feeling that the judge didn't want to make a ruling in such an unprecedented case. It's one thing when someone biologically related to a child is trying to get custody. It's something totally different when there is no relation.

After the break, my mom went up to the stand, and I could sense her anger, hurt, and pain in her voice. Not just from the loss of my daughter, but for me, her own daughter, as well. Only my mom knows the times I called her bawling uncontrollably. The times when I got not-so-great news from the attorney and I was livid. The times when the person she would speak to multiple times per week would no longer call her anymore or answer her calls. The daughter who gained fifty pounds during this whole court battle. The daughter who was no longer recognizable to her. The daughter who lost the spark in her eyes, the daughter that lost the will to go on. This meant more to my mom in ways that no one could even imagine. A mother's worst fear is their child being in some form of pain and there is nothing they can do to make it go away. The whole time leading up to the hearing, I thought it would be my dad that I would have to worry about losing his cool. But in reality, it ended up being my mom. Because we all loved my daughter. No one ever expected to be here. And out of everyone, my mom always treated her father with love and respect even when he did not deserve it. She worked hard to keep the peace between us.

As my mom was up there testifying, she was pulling up pictures from the holidays and other family events. The judge then took a moment to talk about when he interviewed my daughter. He said that she was so cute when he talked to her. He described how her glasses would sit at the bridge of her nose and she would look down at him. He talked about how my daughter talked about all the good times we had and how she misses holidays at Mom-Mom and Pop-Pop's house. Whew, talk about heart wrenching. We all teared up at that moment.

At the end of it all, everyone had their own piece to the puzzle. By the time it was all said and done, the puzzle was just missing one last piece. My piece, of course. But naturally, my piece was the biggest piece of the puzzle. It was time for me to step up and leave it all on the stand. I had a migraine that was throbbing so bad that I couldn't even see straight. I honestly wasn't sure if I was about to stroke out or what. I cried, I sobbed, and I got angry. But then a calming peace came over me, because as I testified about all of the things that I had done for my child, it made me happy. No matter how much he tried to defame, dispute, or tarnish what I had done for her, the facts were the facts, and I had an overwhelming amount of evidence to support what I was stating. At the end of the day, there was no way anyone could deny the huge part I played in her life as her mother. And it was also clear that I met all four criteria of being her psychological parent.

I testified for about an hour. My migraine was throbbing so badly at this point from the stress and anxiety and because I had gone all day without eating because my stomach had been a ball of nerves since the night before. By the time I finished testifying, it was about four p.m., and the court was about to close for the day. I just knew that the judge was going to have us set another court date to continue. However, once I finished testifying, her father then decided he wanted to try to mediate. I was relieved in a sense but also was ready to find out the judge's ruling because the evidence was so overwhelming that there was no way the judge could not rule in my favor. However, a piece of me was also yearning for a resolution, so I agreed to mediate. That was what the whole process was leading up to: a resolution.

So, against my better judgement, I went into mediation without my parents. It was just me, my attorney, and her father. At first, the mediation started out as a dumpster fire. He spent the whole time rehashing our relationship and not focusing on the matter at hand, which was the child. The attorney kept redirecting the conversation to put the focus back on the visitation agreement. At first, he was being totally unreasonable by only wanting me to see her on the weekend with no overnights. It was at this point that I was ready to go back into the courtroom and let the judge rule. However, after much back and forth, we came to an agreement. I think by that time I was just spent and had no more fight in me.

Once we came to an agreement, we went back in to tell the judge. The judge was satisfied with the agreement. I was happy because the hearing ended just in time for her to be able to attend family vacation. Once we were getting ready to leave, her father told me that he would have my daughter call me that evening.

Once we exited out of the courtroom, we all went back into the meeting room, and I just broke down crying. I was so emotional, relieved, mad, and sad all at the same time. I was relieved because I was finally going to be able to see her again. I was mad because it never should've had to come to this. I was saddened because the arrangement I once had was no more. I was so overcome with emotion that my dad had to hold me up because my legs were too weak to stand. I was such a ball of nerves that my mom had to drive me and my car to my parents' house. It was just so surreal.

One would think that it was all over and now everything could go back to normal, right?

Wrong.

I got a call while at my parents' house that same day from his phone, and the first thing I heard when I answered and said hello was, "Hi, Miss Nicki."

I knew that this could not be her on the phone because, before this whole ordeal, I was Mommy. Who could this possibly be on the phone? So I said, "Is this my munchkin?"

She said, "Yes."

Just when I thought my heart couldn't crumble any more, it did. I felt like someone just stabbed me in the heart with the biggest butcher knife. I had to hold my composure together because I did not want the first time that I talked to her after all of these months to be filled with all of my emotions. She sounded so different on the phone. It was like she grew up without me for these seven months. We talked for a little bit, and I knew that I would be seeing her that weekend. So after I calmed down enough from the day's events, I was able to drive myself back home. I just remember lying in the bed with the biggest headache, trying to process everything that happened that day. I remember not getting a wink of sleep that night.

The next day I got up and started fixing everything around my house, putting the pictures back up and going in her room and making sure that everything was set for when she came over. For the most part, her room looked the same way it did when she left. She still had Christmas presents that were not even opened yet because when he took her away, it was so close to Christmas. I made sure that I bought her something for every special occasion I missed. So even though it hurt me, I made sure to buy her something for Valentine's Day, Easter, and her birthday.

So the day was finally here. The day that she was coming over. I left work early that day because I just could not contain my emotions. I was nervous, I was scared, and I was excited all in one. I did not know what to expect. Would she be happy to see me? Would she be mad at me? Would she be sad? Would she be excited? Would she give me a hug when she saw me? Those were all the questions that ran through my head.

As it got closer to six p.m., my heart began to race more and more. She called me and told me she was on her way. So, like a little kid, I kept peeking through my blinds, anticipating her arrival. Finally, she got out of the car, and I saw her smiling and skipping up to the house. That immediately made my heart melt because then I knew she was just as excited as me. She rang the doorbell, and I opened the door. I gave her the biggest hug, and I just started crying. I didn't realize I was squeezing her so tight until she said she couldn't breathe. After I told her how much I missed her, she ran right up to her room, and she was so surprised to see that everything was still the same.

She was so tall, and she looked so different to me. It was like I missed so much of her life the seven months she was gone. We sat in my room on my bed for a little while, and then she asked to take a selfie of us. That made me so happy. I thought to myself, *She still loves me.*

I told her we had an action-packed weekend because there were so many people that wanted to see her. I told her that we were going to go to my parent's house in the morning to see everyone, but she didn't want to wait. So I told my brothers to get over to our parents' house because we were on our way. She talked to me the whole ride there. When we got to the house, she hid behind me because she didn't want anyone to see her. Once we got there and my niece saw her, she immediately started crying. My niece had missed her so much. She was six at the time my daughter was taken. I remember she made a wanted poster for my daughter. That was heartbreaking to see how much she missed her. So that's why I always said this did not only affect me—it affected so many other people in my family.

To this day, the road to reestablishing our relationship still gets difficult at times. I had to release the guilt from it all. Everything that I always did for her was always in her best interest. I also have accepted that our relationship will never go back to what it once was. I also know that if I suffered and hurt this much through this whole ordeal, I can only imagine how she had to process this whole situation herself. For this to happen to a little nine-and ten-year-old girl so abruptly with no explanation, I cannot imagine her level of sadness, discomfort, hurt, and abandonment. I just pray that she knows how much I fought for her and prayed for her while she was gone. And I know there will be a time that I can tell her that although I was ready to give up and end it all, my love for her was far greater, and I could not do that to me or her. I truly believe that as she gets older, she will understand all that me and my family sacrificed for her to still be in our lives.

As descriptive as I tried to be, I still do not think anyone can completely understand how devastating this season of my life was. I was so withdrawn during this time that I barely spoke to anyone. I rarely answered any calls, but the text messages, the inspirational quotes, and the people praying for me (whether known or unknown) was and is still greatly appreciated. But despite it all, I survived, and all it takes is a mustard seed a faith to get you through to the other side. This chapter is a testimony to let you know that when you are facing something that seems impossible to overcome, don't ever give up, and continue to fight, as I learned in this chapter of my life that all you need is a small mustard seed of faith and then watch God work on your behalf.

CHAPTER 2

Heartbreak Hotel

When your desire to be with someone is higher than your self-worth this desire will overrule your intuition in order to keep that person in your life. EVERY...DAMN...TIME.
—Malcolm M.J. Harris

If you would have ever asked me prior to this relationship if I would ever be "that girl" that would take the word of a lying, cheating, no-good man over that of her friends and others, I would've looked at you like you were crazy. However, when you lack self-worth, self-love, and self-awareness, this is when you find yourself in the most compromising positions.

I was finally ready to open myself back up to dating after going to therapy and working on healing my heart—or so I thought. I signed up for an online dating site that I was on back in my early twenties. I didn't really have that much success on it then, but I decided to give it another try since I was older.

I wasn't really having that much success on it until Hassan messaged me. He was handsome, educated, and was working on his doctoral studies. He worked in education like me, so I felt like we had a lot in common, not to mention that he was from my hometown as well. I did not know him growing up because he was much older than me (although I did not find this out until after we started dating). He was seven years older than me, but he lied on his profile and made himself only two years older than me. Who knew that that one red flag in the very beginning would turn into an awful web of lies and deceit?

When we first started dating, I would very rarely go to his house. I worked about forty minutes from where I lived, so I would always have to go directly home after work to pick up my daughter from the after-school program. It was not unusual for me to not go over to his house, and he would always come and visit me. For the first six months or so, I did not let him come over if my daughter was home because I did not want him meeting her if we were not planning to be in a relationship. He gave me a "disclaimer" in the beginning of the relationship that he was very busy, and he said he told women this in the beginning, and they said that they could handle it, and then it would become too much for them to handle. Once again, here was another red flag that I chose to ignore. In his defense, he was in the midst of completing his doctoral studies. As I went through this myself, I knew how demanding a doctoral program could be. I wanted to show him how much of a committed girlfriend I could be, and I promised to help him through this program.

Now, in my mind, I thought of myself as being a supportive girlfriend, but because I lacked self-awareness, I didn't realize that I was falling into the same pattern of my relationships, which was overexerting myself by helping my partner at the detriment to myself. See, this is what happens when you don't love or see the worth in yourself. I was constantly looking for that external validation because I did not see it in myself. I always thought that if I showed men how valuable I am, how smart I am, then they would have no choice but to see the worth in me, right? Wrong! Having this extreme need to always prove my worth to men never did anything but cause me extreme hurt in the end because the reality was men could sense that I didn't love myself from a mile away. And unfortunately, the men that I chose throughout my life chose to do nothing more than to capitalize off of this.

I believed every empty promise that he ever told me. He would tell me how I was his "future everything," the "love of his life," and how he was so thankful to have me in his life. I hung on every broken promise of how once he finally finished with his doctoral studies that we would spend so much more time together. I believed everything he said because I wanted it so bad. I loved the idea of us being together. The thought of a "power couple" in the field of education both with doctorate degrees was so inspiring to me. I let the thoughts of what could be cause me to ignore everything else that was wrong right before my eyes.

I slowly started noticing little things that I just chalked up to me overreacting. Things such as I would only really talk to him while he was in his car. And when I would talk to him on his way home from work, once he got home, he would always say, "Let me get all of these bags in the house and I will call you back," and of course that call would never come unless he was back in his car later that evening.

Another red flag was that he would rarely answer his phone when I would call him, and especially when I called him at night, he would never answer the phone. He would always tell me how he fell asleep early or that his ringer was still on silent from earlier in the day. And even though this didn't sit right with my spirit, I still chose to believe him. I would often send him vile texts after he didn't answer, and then of course he would call back. Not to mention I could always tell when someone was around him because the way he would talk to me would change. When he was in the car, I was "babe this," "babe that," and being called "beautiful" and "the love of his life." But clearly when he was around someone, it was almost like we were on a business call. It was so impersonal, but yet again I never said anything.

Time after time after time I knew he wasn't being completely honest with me, and yet I did not love myself enough to do anything about it, because at that time, in my mind, having a piece of something was better than having nothing at all. And the sad part was he knew this too. He used my lack of worth to his advantage to score big. I offered to guide him through the dissertation process because, like I said before, since I had already been through this process, I knew that writing a dissertation was not for the faint of heart. I went from proofreading his chapter one to damn near writing his entire dissertation for him. He was a horrible writer so this was no easy task. I wrote his acknowledgments section, I transcribed all of his data for the results chapter of his dissertation, I added in citations and completed his chapters four and five, I completed the Institutional Review Board (IRB) process for him for his school. The IRB is an administrative body of colleges and universities established to protect the rights and welfare of human research subjects recruited to participate in research activities. I basically wrote a second dissertation because I did everything for him. And I just knew that by me coming through for him in such a major way that he would finally see me and want to be with me forever. But for someone who is a master manipulator, it was just another way for him to get ahead.

As if it wasn't enough that I had my own red flags, I had people coming up to me telling me things about him as well. Like I said earlier, being as though we were from the same town, it was inevitable that someone would know him. I had so many people telling me things about him. My best friend Ashanti met me for lunch one day to tell me that he was talking to one of her friends. He was basically feeding her the same lines he was feeding me, that once he finished his dissertation, he was going to have more time for her. And when he and I went to a comedy show one weekend, he told her that he went with his "boys." Like, who does that? I even talked to the girl on the phone, trying to get a better understanding of what was going on (something else that I said I would never do). And of course when I confronted him, he denied everything. He even went on to say how "ugly" she was and he would never be attracted to someone like her. Meanwhile, the only person who was ugly was him because he had such an ugly spirit. In hindsight, I know that he was using her too because her mother was helping him save his house because he was underwater on his mortgage and about to lose his home. Once again, he kept people around that he could benefit from.

I also had two other friends that had a connection to him indirectly. The way everyone was connected is too complex to explain, but all I know is that every week I was getting information fed to me about him. It was so bad that even his ex-fiancée offered to talk to me to let me know how much of a dog he really was, but for whatever reason, at the time, I was not ready to face the truth that I already knew. My friend Dana and others would tell me that he was living with someone, that he was using me because I would give him anything he wanted, that he was telling people we were only business partners, and basically everyone was laughing at how dumb I was being. And in the end, all of it was true.

One thing was true. We did establish a business partnership. But once again I did all of the work, I came up with the name, filed the paperwork with the state, created our website, and also looked for opportunities for us to consult. So back in 2017, he and I flew out to Los Angeles to present at a national conference. Of course, I wrote and submitted the proposal and made all of the arrangements in preparation for travel. He paid me for his plane ticket but never paid me for the hotel room.

It just so happened that my older brother was also in LA during the same time for work. Hassan told his ex-fiancée and others that although we were presenting together, he had his own room and I was staying in my brother's room. This was certainly not the truth because Hassan and I shared a room together the whole trip. When this information got back to me, I said to myself, "How would his ex-fiancée know that my brother was in LA unless he told her?" He played me for a fool time and time again, and it is so true what people say about men. Once they know they can do you wrong with no consequences, it is a wrap, and they will continue to do so until you reach a point of realization that you know you deserve better.

One thing that I was always too embarrassed to tell anyone about was intimacy or lack thereof. How is it that two people can be together for over four years and never be intimate? The whole time we were together, we were intimate only twice. Yes, you read that right. Twice! He blamed it on stress from his job, stress from the doctoral program, and just overall being depressed and not in the mind frame of wanting to be intimate, but he always assured me that it had nothing to do with me. How could I talk to any of my girls about this? Because I knew they would do nothing but confirm what I already knew. He was not having sex with me because he was clearly getting it from someone else. There were times that we traveled together and would be in the same hotel room, and there would be no intimacy. We traveled to the Poconos, Washington, DC, Los Angeles, and Maryland, and each time there was no intimacy. But what was consistent was that he would always leave the room to go smoke each and every night. I would say to myself, "I know he is going outside to call his girlfriend." I would often say to myself while in tears, "Come on, Nicole, how much more of this are you willing to take?" One time I even packed something sexy to wear, and he was gone so long that by the time he came back in, I was beyond tired and so hurt that I didn't want to be bothered at all.

The only person I ever had the courage to ever say anything to was my older brother, Jeff. And although he was grossed out by the thought of the topic of his sister and sex, he assured me that Hassan was most definitely getting it from someone else. He said that there was no way in the world a man was going four years without sex. He told me then I should leave him. Of course no brother ever wants to see their sister hurt. Jeff would always say to me that he just didn't trust him. He said that Hassan was always too quiet. My brother would tell me that Hassan never talked much because he did not want to have to try to keep his lies straight. My brother would tell me that no one is that nice. And that's another thing, he met everyone in my family: my parents, my daughter, my brothers. I only met his mother and sister one time, and that one time was at his graduation. And the funny thing is he never introduced me as his girlfriend. His mother and sister already knew about me but only as the person that worked so hard to get him across the finish line of completing his dissertation. His mother was so grateful for how I supported him, but he never told them any more about me.

When I was going through the situation with my daughter, he was not sympathetic or empathetic at all. At the lowest point in my life, when I was lost, hopeless, and just full of despair, I would ask him to spend the night with me repeatedly, and he never would. He blamed me for being someone he "hated" talking to when I was depressed. He was one of the main advocates of me to just "let it go" and move on with my life. This was the only time that I would get livid with him and go off. And in hindsight, I wasn't even defending my honor—I was defending my daughter's. Why didn't I love myself enough to defend my own honor?

He was supposed to be the one to have my back the most during this time, and he could not even take time out of his life to check on me. Instead, he would use the excuse of I was unpleasant to be around and he didn't know how to support me. So I was completely alone.

Each time that I got another piece of the puzzle should've been enough to make me leave, but none of it was ever the piece to make me walk away. Because, honestly, who else would want me? A woman who was morbidly obese, in a deep depression, and did not even like the reflection she saw in the mirror.

Then the day came that everything truly unfolded. And when I say unfolded, I mean to the point that there was no denying anything. In May 2018, I bought him tickets to the Sixers game for

Father's Day, and this was the first time in a while that I got dressed up and actually liked who was staring back at me in the mirror.

We decided to go grab something to eat prior to the game. As I was pulling into the parking lot, I got a call from a number I didn't recognize. I ignored it because I thought it was a robocall, and I figured if it was important, that person would leave a message. Oh, how I wish I would've answered that call (you will understand why later).

He then got a call and told me to go inside and get a table and he would be right in. I went inside, got a table, and ordered a drink. I waited for him for about fifteen minutes. Finally, he came in with this distraught look on his face. I asked him what was wrong. He said that his grandfather went missing again. Now, this wasn't too far-fetched, as he explained to me in the past that his grandfather had dementia and would often wander out on his own. Being that one of my grandmothers passed away from this horrible disease, I know how stressful it can be, so I never questioned it.

He claimed that he needed to get back to his car immediately and assist in the search party.

At this point, I was angry because I just knew this was not true at all. We were driving back to my house so that he could get his car, and I remember just yelling at him and telling him he had better pay me back for these tickets, and he kept apologizing profusely and saying he was going to make it up to me. At this point, he had so many IOUs stacked up I could not even keep count anymore. He was constantly letting me down and never making it up. He was constantly letting me down and never making it up because I was allowing him to.

We pulled up to my house and got out of the car, and he tried to kiss me. I kept walking past him like I didn't see him, and I went in the house. No more than two seconds after I put my purse down on the couch, I got a text. A text from the same number that called me earlier. And the text read: "I don't know who Hassan is to you, but I have been with him for eight years, and you need to tell him to bring his butt home."

It was like my whole body went numb. It went numb for several reasons. At thirty-eight years old, was I really dealing with having another girl calling me on my phone asking me who I was to her man? Did he really lie on his sick grandfather and use him as an excuse to get back to his girlfriend in fear of her blowing everything up? Did it really take for *this* to happen in order for me to accept what I already knew? Why didn't I answer the phone when I saw this call? So many questions were running through my mind.

Of course I immediately called him and told him the piece of shit he was. All he could say was he would explain later. What the hell could there possibly be to explain? The gig was up, and everything that I suspected was confirmed. He kept saying, "Whatever you do, just do not answer her calls or call her back." At the end of the day, I had to face reality that I was his side chick. And there was no disputing that.

She called me back, and I answered, and we talked on the phone. She went on about how she knew everything about me and how she was going to call and invite me to lunch to show me the "receipts" (evidence, in layman's terms) on him. What bothered me the most about the whole situation was she knew everything about me. She knew where I lived, where I worked; she knew about my kid. It was just too much. But because she approached me respectfully, I did not feel the need to be disrespectful. But I let her know that I did not have any interest in meeting her for lunch, as I now knew all that I needed to know. It was more about her trying to convince me to leave him alone more than anything else. I also let her know that if it wasn't me, it would be someone else. That was who he was: an opportunist that looked to get all he could from women—especially from women who don't see their worth. Instead of calling me, she should have been having this conversation with him, because as much as he had no respect for me, he had none for her either.

I called him back after speaking to her, and of course, in typical fashion, he tried to deflect and get angry at me because I did not listen to him when he told me not to contact her. It was classic manipulation at its finest. I saw a new side of him at that time. Anyone who could use his ailing grandfather as a reason to be a disgusting cheating dog is the lowest of the low. And at that point, I was good.

I hung up on him, and I called my best friend Aqsa. I was so overcome with emotion that I could not even formulate a sentence. I was crying hysterically on the phone trying to put together words to explain to her what happened. Because Aqsa and I worked together, she knew a lot of what I was dealing with. I had so much embarrassment and shame as I was telling her what happened. How could I be that girl? How could I be that one who ignored my gut? How could I hate myself that much that I accepted this for four years? How could I not recognize that I deserve better? I was so ashamed from this.

Aqsa wanted to come over and keep me company, but I did not want her to come. The embarrassment was becoming too much of a burden to bear. I told her I would be OK, even though I knew I was lying. I took a sleeping pill and went to bed early that night. That was the only way I could sleep. I am a thinker, so once my brain is locked in on overthink mode, that brings nothing but sleepless nights for me.

I could not even bring myself to call my mom the day it happened. My God, she was still fresh off of having to keep me together from the situation with my daughter. I could not possibly have her worrying about me again. But I knew that I was in my cycle of overthinking again, so I called her the next day when I was feeling better. Or at least so I thought, because as soon as she said hello, I just started crying again. Of course, being the person she is, she went right into mama bear mode, and she was ready to seek and destroy. And in the same sentence, my mom wouldn't be my mom if she also didn't give me an ounce of truth. And the truth was, I knew this all along. She was right I did. She remembered when I came to her house the day I drove past his house and saw two cars parked outside, another thing that I never thought I would do, but there I was. She knew all of the information that others brought to me, and yet I tried to rationalize in my mind how this could not be true.

It was so hurtful to sit here and write this chapter and relive all that I chose to ignore. There was a quote that I read one day that says, "Whatever you are not changing, you are choosing." In hindsight, I wanted to blame him for all of the hurt that he caused me. I wanted to make him out to be this villain and I was just a victim. I wanted to get back at him by reporting him to his school and telling the real truth about who really wrote his dissertation. But the raw truth is, I chose this. I chose not to trust my gut; I chose not to see the situation for what it really was. I chose not to fully be vulnerable in therapy so that we could really get to the root cause of why I didn't love myself. I chose all of this. So as a result, I chose to be cheated on, lied to, manipulated, and used. As much as I wanted to scream from the mountaintop that I was innocent in this, I was not. I was guilty of not seeing the queen that stood before me. And as you can see, that cost me dearly.

CHAPTER 3

Career Confusion

Choose a job you love and you will never have to work a day in your life.
—Confucius

Normally when people are going through tough times in their personal lives, they use work as a distraction. Well, what do you do when work is also one of the major sources of stressors in your life too? That's where I found myself, in complete and utter turmoil. There was no place I could turn where I could find a reprieve. I hated coming to work, I hated going home, and more importantly, I hated myself. Home was nothing more than a reminder of what I lacked, work was stressful, and I felt undervalued and unappreciated.

I started a position at a community college in July 2013. Ironically, I graduated with my doctorate degree in May 2013, only to find out that the school district that I worked in for seven years was abolishing my position in June 2013 and I would be out of a job.

I have always prided myself on accomplishing all goals that I set for myself. For me, career goals were no different. I always knew that I wanted to start my own business. My mother and I started a business several years ago, and we were even profitable within our first year in business. It was like we were the dynamic duo. We were a match made in heaven. However, my mom took a leadership position, so we were unable to keep many of the contracts we had due to a conflict of interests. And as a result, things kind of stalled.

I was not unemployed for long. I was laid off in June 2013, and I was able to land a position as the assistant director of grants for a local community college. Things were looking up for me. This was my first position in higher education, so I was excited to gain experience in this realm. Within the first six months of me being in the position, I was promoted to director of grants. I was very happy. I was gaining great experience in writing grants at the higher-ed level, I was managing staff, and I got to be a part of some great initiatives at the college as well as working under some great women.

Three years into my tenure working at the college, I learned that they would be rolling out a new initiative that was very innovative and was going to bring great resources to residents in the region. I was very excited about it at first, and with this new initiative came another promotion. I had more responsibility, and I was able to learn more about workforce development. I was thankful for this opportunity. I felt like this was where I belonged. The college had recently hired a minority president. There was more diversity among the staff. I honestly felt that I could see myself there for a long time working my way up the career ladder.

However, in 2017, things took a turn for the worst. There was a lot of transition within the department I worked for. I was dealing with the situation with my daughter, a relationship that wasn't genuine and full of lies and deceit, depression, and a host of other emotions that I previously talked about. It was almost as if my mind and heart could not handle anything else.

But somehow that didn't matter because a shit storm ensued at work. I became involved in an investigation that did not directly involve me. I, however, was indirectly involved. And although I will not share the details of the incident, it caused me extreme levels of anxiety and stress for months. And to make matters worse, I received no support or guidance from my leadership or HR. I was forced to deal with this situation on my own. Because of the nature of the incident, I was not allowed to talk to anyone about it. I was forced to deal with this situation the best way I knew how.

I was at this point going to therapy once a week because this was the only way that I could cope. Between my personal life and work life, it was in complete shambles. There were times where I felt like I could come in and flip my desk over. There were times that I would go out to my car and cry because the stress became entirely too much to carry.

What made it worse was that no one knew what I was dealing with with my daughter at work. People would ask me how she was doing, and I would lie, all the while trying not to crumble from the thoughts of her and really not knowing how she was doing. I was living a double life. And that in itself was beyond exhausting; I did not know how to cope with all that I was going through. I remember on many different occasions I would wonder what it would be like if I were no longer here.

If I were just unable to feel anymore, I felt like that would just be so much better than the internal warfare I would experience day after day.

Things at work just kept getting worse and worse. The internal investigation that had been ongoing was ramping up. I was being questioned often regarding certain events that transpired. I was being asked questions that made me uncomfortable and about things that I had no knowledge about. I felt like my professionalism was being questioned. And that bothered me more than anything. My integrity is important to me. And I felt like I was under the microscope as well for a situation that I had nothing to do with. And again, I had no one to talk to about this. I was out on an island by myself. The person who I thought was my dear friend I did not recognize anymore. And although I understand that the situation created a barrier for us, I just felt like my feelings were never considered the whole time.

The chain of events was unreal. I literally concluded my case in family court in August 2017. No more than a few days later, this suit was filed by one of my former employees/friends. I went from one stressful situation right into the next. My mind and heart were still reeling from the emotional roller coaster that I was on for the past seven months. In my mind, I was thinking I could not possibly handle anything else at this point. The only silver lining to this entire moment was when the suit was filed with my job—it was on a Friday. That next week I was going on vacation with my family, including my daughter. I knew that I was not going to be there for the initial fallout, which was a godsend. I wanted to enjoy my time with family, so I completely unplugged from work. However, I knew what was going to be waiting for me when I got back.

When I returned from vacation, things at work were so awkward. People were being pulled in for questioning regarding the situation, which created a dark cloud over the workplace. And although I knew what was going on, none of us would dare say anything to each other about it, although we wanted to. It was like we were sworn to secrecy, almost to the point that if we discussed the particulars of what was going on, we would be terminated. That was a crazy position to put people in. We had no choice in the matter. We were forced to be in this position and then had no outlet to vent. I hated coming to work every day. I felt like I went from one shitty situation to the next. I was hoping that I was going to have a chance to kind of process my new normal and try to gain some semblance of peace. But that was not going to happen. I felt like I went from the frying pan to the fire with absolutely no warning. I would often ask myself, "Is the devil testing me to see how long it will actually take me to have a nervous breakdown or, more importantly, just end it all?"

My work was suffering. I spent the majority of my day managing personnel issues, trying to keep people motivated when I myself was the furthest from motivated, having my hands tied behind my back and not being able to ask for work to be completed by the person who started the investigation but having people jump down my throat because they felt I was letting her get away with murder. From their point of view, I totally understood why they felt that way. But they didn't know that I was told that I had to be hands off. And as a result, I was taking on two roles. The fact that I was overworked, disregarded, and disengaged just made coming to work damn near impossible.

Once again, it was nothing but prayer and therapy that got me through. I was taking off more time than usual. I needed mental health days at least once a week. But no one ever checked in with me to see how I was holding up through this whole ordeal. I had the weight of the organization on my shoulders, and not one person seemed to care. It was at this point that I realized that my employer did not value their employees—and more specifically, me. I knew that it was time for me to start looking for employment elsewhere. And although I knew this, I just did not have the mental fortitude to start looking. I was just dealing with entirely too much.

After about nine months, the case was finally settled, and I thought things were going to calm down and I could try to get myself together and heal from this storm. But I was sadly mistaken. This case caused the department I was in to become heavily scrutinized. And with this scrutinization came a reorganization for the whole department. I went from being a director to a manager. And I was supposed to be OK with it because they wanted our titles to more closely align with the county. Like, how was that supposed to make me feel better? I went from having a position I loved to a position I absolutely hated. And I went to reporting to a new supervisor for the third time. The morale in my department was already low. This just made it that much worse. I would often talk to people who also received a title change, and we would just vent with each other. How was I supposed to be happy when I got screwed over? Not to mention that after everything was said and done, no one ever acknowledged what I went through and how I did my best to remain professional and keep the morale of my team high. I am not saying that I expected a trophy or anything, but just a simple thank you or being shown some form of appreciation would have meant so much to me. But that never came.

I went from having a supervisor that gave me the autonomy to grow and flourish in my position to being micromanaged. To add insult to injury, I was the *only* person in my department with a terminal degree. I am talking about out of a team of fifty employees. I was the only one with a doctorate degree. I never worked for a place, especially an educational institution, where there was no value placed on credentials.

I can own that I had a learning curve when I started my new role in workforce development. But I also knew that I had enough background knowledge and experience that it would've been able to sustain me. But none of that mattered: I was constantly checked up on, my work calendar was heavily monitored, I was not allowed to effectively supervise my staff, and I had to constantly document my progress on things. I often questioned why they wanted me there. I was way more valuable than what they were using me for.

Once again, my work began to suffer, and I was beyond disengaged. I actively started pursuing other opportunities. I was making it my responsibility that, although I would come home tired and emotionally drained, I still needed to apply for at least two jobs a night and at the same time continue to build my business. This often meant late nights for me, but I knew that it had to be done. I was turning into someone I did not recognize anymore. I would often come into work disgruntled, and I was not the friendliest person anymore. The way I dressed started to change. Whereas I used to always come to work dressed to the nines with matching accessories, that stopped. I just didn't care.

The best part of this career confusion that I was experiencing was that it allowed me to meet some of my closest friends and make some amazing connections with people I would not have necessarily crossed paths with. Although I lost "friends" as a result of working at the college, God saw fit to replace them with something better. I gained people who were more than just co-workers, and I am so thankful for them. And without these people in my life, I would've walked off of the job a long time ago. These people prayed for and with me, laughed with me, went to happy hour with me, and let me cry and vent to them.

In my quest of finding a better job, I started applying for any- and everything. I went on several interviews, but none of them made me feel like that was where I was supposed to be. And the last thing I wanted to do was take a position out of desperation and be equally as miserable if not more as I was now.

So I waited. I waited until I found something that would feed my passion. Something that I lost at the college a long time ago.

And then finally it happened. I had always wanted to work in the criminal justice system, so I applied for a couple of jobs, and I finally got a call. And when I went to this interview, it was just different. I felt confident, and I was able to market myself in a way that I never did before. I felt like I knocked the interview out of the park. And I did just that. I received a call two months later saying that I was the candidate of choice. I was so happy. It was more money, more leadership responsibility, and it was giving me a chance to work with youth in the juvenile justice system. An added bonus was the leadership team was very diverse, something that I had been seeking for so long. I no longer wanted the days of being the only minority in the room. I was tired of explaining to people who did not look like me how it felt to feel like an outcast simply because of the color of your skin.

I want nothing more to be a part of an organization that values me as an employee and knows and appreciates what I bring to the table. I want to work for people who are not intimidated by my talents and abilities and totally want to see me flourish.

I want to leave you with this: don't ever feel that you are "stuck" at a job. If you don't feel passionate about what you do, if you feel like you are being kept in a box, and if you are emotionally, physically, or mentally drained after a day of work, trust and believe me it will not get better. We can't make people change, but what we can do is change the situation. Please do not ever stay in a job that doesn't feed your passion. And if you cannot find this in a job, then create it for yourself. Because at the end of the day, no one is going to believe in you more than you believe in yourself. So start that business, start that blog, write that book, start selling your creations. Start doing whatever brings you the greatest joy. I know I did, and now that I have, there is no turning back.

CHAPTER 4

Fair-Weather Friends

Lots of people want to ride with you in the limo, but what you want is someone who will take the bus with you when the limo breaks down.
—Oprah Winfrey

My grandmother would always say that you can count your true friends on one hand. I never knew that to be true until recently. It is so true what they say: you never know who your true friends are until you go through something devastating. This is when your true friends will reveal themselves.

I can own that through this dark storm in my life, I was not the easiest person to deal with. But true friends know this and will do their very best to support you even if they don't know how. During the years 2017 and 2018 when I was dealing with everything, I was severely withdrawn. I would look at my phone and see someone calling but just would not have the strength to answer the phone. People would text me and ask if I was home, and I would lie and say no even though I was.

I rarely went out on the weekends. I would just stay home, lie on the couch, eat myself sick, and just be numb. There were so many things that I was dealing with at once. The loss of my daughter, being in a relationship with a no-good man, a job that wasn't doing anything but making me feel even more worthless. And then there were friends that I thought would have my back through it all, but I quickly learned that this was not the case.

I had "friends" tell me that maybe my relationship with my daughter had come to an end and that I should be glad that I had more free time to "do me." That thought never crossed my mind and I did not feel that way at all. Anyone who was a true friend to me knew what she meant to me. Someone who could be so insensitive to say something like this to me was not a friend at all. It took everything in me not to completely unleash rage on the people who said this to me. However, I was grounded just enough to know if I responded to this comment that I would unleash the full wrath of all I was carrying on these people and that would be something that I would not be able to bounce back from. I chose to digress instead.

To add to this, there were many people who knew the real situation with my daughter, but there were just as many that didn't. So those who were closest to me knew the real deal from day one when she was taken away, and I leaned on them heavily. However, there were many that I was living a lie with. For the people who did not know the real truth regarding my situation with my daughter, they believed she was my biological daughter.

When months went by and she still was not back in my life, I felt like I needed to come clean and tell people the truth. Most people were amazing through this situation. A lot of them were mad at me that I thought that they would be mad at me when I told them the truth. A lot of them spoke to my bond with my daughter because they said if I never told them that she was not biologically mine, they would've never known because all they knew was that we loved each other.

Specifically, my best friends Bianca and Zahirah were upset with me because I thought they would be mad when I finally told them the truth. It's very hard when you start out as co-workers because you are never sure where things will go. So you go along with your typical story because that is much easier than going through the motions of my particular situation, especially when you are unsure of the roles these people will play in your life initially.

Bianca has always been no nonsense to the point that I always knew that I needed to have bail money readily available (jokingly, of course…maybe) because she always had a short fuse for foolishness. When I initially told Bianca, she was ready to roll some people out. Bianca will always be a ride-or-die type of friend.

And when I told Zahirah, she came from such a place of love that I was mad that I waited so long to tell her. We were not friends for that long at this time, so I honestly wasn't sure how she would receive it. She cried as I told her and was honored that I trusted her enough to even share this part of my life with her, and that was how I knew that she was a true friend.

My friend Sanja was very supportive as well. Our daughters were in dance class together. So when my daughter stopped showing up to dance class in the middle of the year I felt like I needed to tell her. She was so shocked when I told her. She prayed for me all the time and she kept a very positive attitude about my daughter returning home. She would always say when your daughter comes back home we have to get our girls together. I will always be forever grateful for how she believed my daughter would be back home soon even when I didn't always believe it.

However, there were some who did not understand why I was not completely truthful with them from the beginning. I had my reasoning, whether they were coworkers at the time or people whom I met within the last couple of years. I just didn't feel that it was important for me to share this with them initially. I am naturally a private person, so I didn't think that our friendships would grow to the place that I needed to even disclose this information to them. When they chose to respond unfavorably, in my mind, all of these negative responses would swirl around in my head, but I chose not to let those vile words hit my lips. I was thinking to myself at the most devastating point in my life, "You want to make it about yourself that you didn't know the whole story." It was at that point that I knew these people had weeded themselves out of my life. Because there was no way that I would ever forget that moment. Furthermore, I knew that I had a very grudgeful side, and I knew that I would hold a grudge on them for how they responded. At that point, it was just better for me to walk away from those so-called friendships.

I also lost someone whom I considered to be a big sister to me behind a work-related incident. That really bothered me because when I care about someone, I put my all into the friendship/relationship. I felt like I did not mean as much to her as she meant to me. Because once the dust settled at the job, I felt like she didn't need me in her life anymore, and the conversations happened less and less. It took me a while to get over that one. But I am a firm believer of when God removes something or someone from your life, he will replace it with something greater. And although my tenure at the college I worked for was not all good, I am thankful for all of the amazing friendships I formed because of that job.

Now let me also say that in this chapter of my life I was not the best friend to people either. I chose the lies of a dog of a man over my friends. I made some of the dumbest decisions and became a very messy, gossipy individual all in the name of "love." I would have never thought in a million years that I would be that woman who would think that *all* of my friends were lying and take the word of a man over them. Even though I had all the proof in the world to substantiate everything to the contrary, I still chose to stay and believe his lies. And as a result of all of the foolishness and games, I lost some friends because of them. I violated the trust of some people. And for that I was very ashamed. At that point, I realized I had to take ownership for my part in the demise of some of my friendships.

I became so engrossed in the drama because it was an escape from my reality. If I was consumed with the business of others, then I would not have to deal with my own shit going on. This is how I would justify things in my mind. As skewed as this thinking was, I just went along with it because it beat the alternative of always thinking about the loss of my daughter, the job I hated, how I hated how I looked, and how I hated the fact that I was accepting less than I deserved in a relationship but still didn't do anything about it.

From the beginning of my "relationship" with Hassan, I was being brought back information by friends. Some of it I asked for, and some of it I didn't. It seemed as if every other day I was being told something about Hassan. And every time I was told something, I would confront him about it. And of course, he would lie each time.

My friend Dana, whom I knew since childhood—I am talking twenty-five years—was one of the ones closest to this situation. She had firsthand knowledge on everything. She would often ask me why I didn't ever go to his house and told me that I needed to make it my business to spend more time at his house. She told me that he lived with someone and that his ex would be clowning me because I was being so dumb. And even though I knew that I was being dumb, it wasn't enough to make me stop at the time. I even went as far as to break girl code one time with her because she told me something that her boyfriend told her, and I was not supposed to repeat it, but I went right back to my no-good dog and confronted him on it. The crazy part is that deep down inside I knew that everything I was being told was true. But I still chose to deny it. Dana told me that he was telling people that I was just his "business partner." And although I was acting like I lost all my marbles, she never judged me. I almost lost a great friend in Dana because I chose to be so damn messy behind a man. But what I can say about Dana is that she will always speak her truth. And she confronted me on my shit through email. I had no choice but to own my shit and apologize. It just so happened that we were going to a brunch about a year later that allowed for us to have about an hour car ride there and back. I was able to really sincerely apologize to her at this time. We talked about how we had all done some dumb shit behind a man, and we hugged it out.

My best friend Ashanti took me to lunch one day to let me know that my man was seeing someone else. She had details that could not be disputed. I wanted to believe her. I should've believed her. But every part of me wanted her to be wrong. We have been friends for twenty-plus years and have formed a sisterhood. Why would she lie? She even set it up to the point where I spoke to the girl. And although I was acting like I didn't have any sense, I had enough sense not to come at her in a crazy way. Because ultimately my problem was not with her—it was with him. I took the information and even thanked her in the end. Ashanti never judged me for staying with him. She always said that she would support me no matter what. Once I got my head clear from all of the bullshit he put me through, I owed her the biggest apology, and that's just what I did. I believe that this situation made us closer.

Thank God for forgiveness, is all I have to say. I learned so much about myself and others during this dark time in my life. And although I lost many friends during this dark time, I gained some true, genuine friends during this time as well. And I always felt like my friends were supposed to fit a certain criterion, but I learned that this is definitely not true. Some of my closest friends are several years younger than me or several years older than me. One of my closest friends is of the opposite sex. I have learned to trust again through these new genuine friendships I have formed.

Although I have experienced my share of fair-weather "friends," friends who took advantage of our friendship in the workplace, friends who used me for what they could gain, or friends who never had my best interest at heart, I also have some forever friends as well. I can never truly thank those who were there for me during my darkest days. And I wish I could name every single one of you in this book, but you all know who you are. There are no words that can ever express those who loved me when I was the most unlovable. Those who prayed for me when I didn't even know they were doing so. Those who kept me going every day at work with our daily email chat. My friends Sherron and Dana kept my mind so preoccupied during this season in my life. I looked forward to the daily email chats at work because I knew that this was my daily escape from everything that was going wrong in my life. Those laughs were a huge distraction for me. Those who kept reaching out despite the many unanswered calls especially Angel, Tara and Ashanti. My friends Ashley, Bianca, Natika and Takia who were all dealing with their own personal storms in their lives at the time but still took the time out to call and email me to make sure that I was ok. Those who were ready to stomp people out for me, and I mean that in every sense of the word. I am so grateful to have some pretty amazing people in my life. I am not sure that I will ever be able to sincerely thank them. The more I think about it, I didn't really lose anything because I gained a whole hell of a lot more.

CHAPTER 5

Weight Woes

To change your body, you first must change your mind.
—Unknown

For the majority of my life, I can remember being overweight. I was overweight as a child, and because of that I never really felt good about myself. My parents were at the helm of a youth track club organization for over twenty-five years, so I was always surrounded by track athletes. People who were always in shape and skinny. I never fit in. I was always seen as the funny fat girl, but that was it. Nothing more, nothing less. I felt like no one ever saw me as beautiful. Hell, I never saw myself as beautiful. All throughout my life I was smart (all honors and AP classes), involved in a lot of activities (band, dance, clubs, track and field); however, none of that mattered because I felt like all anyone ever saw was my weight. I never really had boyfriends growing up. From early on in my childhood, I tied beauty to outward appearance. And as a result, because I was fat I was not beautiful.

I also struggled with my weight all throughout my adulthood as well. I had a brief stint of being in shape when I went away for undergrad and went to Florida State University on a track and field scholarship. However, losing that weight did not come easy. My workout regimen consisted of two-a-day practices, lifting weights every day, and a lot of running. I remember my first semester there. I had lost about fifty pounds in four months. I remember coming home for Christmas break in 1998 and going back up to my high school, and everyone was looking at me different. I felt like for the first time people saw me as more than just Nicki who was funny as hell. I did not just lose weight, but I was very muscular as well. At eighteen years old, I actually felt confident and beautiful. However, this was short lived.

I competed up until my senior year, in which I then learned that I had two crushed disks in my back that caused major back issues for me. I wasn't able to work out or compete; I saw a chiropractor on a regular basis and was also doing physical therapy. And, of course, because I was not working out like I used to, the weight crept back slowly but surely.

I will never forget the day that my college sweetheart told me that he missed the muscle definition in my legs. And shortly after that we broke up. All throughout my life it was reinforced that beauty was tied to size. I was still the same person that laughed with him all the time and supported him through all of his endeavors. But the minute that I gained back my weight, all of that other stuff didn't matter. At least that was what I told myself.

After graduating from undergrad, I was going to stay in Florida. I had a full-time job working for a school district. But I took the breakup with my college sweetheart very hard, so I moved back to New Jersey. I started working while living with my parents. And this was when my roller-coaster dieting began. I tried any and everything under the sun. Basically, I tried everything but illegal drugs. From Nutrisystem, Weight Watchers, detoxing, cabbage soup diet, and phentermine, the list is exhaustive. I would lose a good amount of weight, but the minute I would stop, I would gain it all back plus more. At the time, I never knew that my battle with my weight was the result of a larger issue.

As I got older, I started to have a little more confidence in myself. But I still did not see myself the way others saw me. People would always tell me how beautiful I was. I would always question what they saw in me to make them think that I was beautiful. I was able to recognize small things about myself that I thought were beautiful, such as my smile and my skin. I started attending parties for BBW (Big Beautiful Women). This was where I truly felt accepted. This was where I learned that just because I was plus size, that did not mean that I would never be desired. And although I learned that there, it still wasn't enough because, ultimately, I did not love myself at all. I was always inspired by the women that were much bigger than me and yet had all the confidence in the world.

Fast forward to 2017, where I was the biggest I have ever been. I was over 340 pounds, in which 50 of those pounds I gained in a year. Between the deep depression I was in, the loss of my daughter, a loveless relationship, and a job I hated, there I stood: the unhealthiest I've been in my life. But at that point, I just did not care. I had zero motivation to do anything. I would come home day after day and just sit, eat, and be sedentary. My will to live, be healthy, and be around others was just gone.

It wasn't until the court case was over and my so-called relationship completely fell apart that I realized I had to do something. I decided in 2018 to go to a weight-loss surgery information session again. I went once before with my mother a few years ago, but I was nowhere near ready mentally at that time. However, this time when I went it felt different. I was committed to finally taking my life back. I listened to three surgeons speak at this information session, and I made an appointment with the surgeon that most resonated with me. And from there, I had to embark on a very comprehensive journey.

This surgery was life saving in more ways than one. In conjunction with my other health issues, I also learned that I had blood pressure so high that the doctor was shocked that I didn't have a constant headache and that I did not stroke out. I was immediately put on high blood pressure medication. I was also diagnosed with sleep apnea, and I was prediabetic. Also, when I went to see the cardiologist, I had an abnormal EKG and had to get an ultrasound of my heart. I often thank God for me going through with this process because if I didn't, who knows how long I might have made it before dying.

I had to also meet with a psychologist to be cleared prior to being approved for surgery. She asked a lot of questions to make sure that I was doing this for the right reason. I am so thankful that I was already in therapy because if I weren't, I do not think that she would have approved me. I was definitely doing this surgery for myself. I also had to see a nutritionist as well. I had one of the coolest surgeons for this whole process. His only requirement was not to gain weight during the three-month process. I was doing well and following all of the recommendations from my nutritionist. I finally felt like I was in a good space.

Then things went off track. While I was preparing for the two-week pre-op diet prior to surgery, my former coworker and best friend, Chris, and I struggled with not being able to do happy hours anymore after work. We enjoyed nothing more than going to our favorite spots for happy hour and overindulging with drinks and appetizers. We would oftentimes worry if our relationship would still be the same, since we would no longer be able to bond over food the way we used to. We ate everything we wanted every day. At no point during the whole food tour did I think that I could be possibly gaining weight. And it hit me like a ton of bricks when I went in for my final weigh-in before my two-week pre-op diet and I saw the scale and I had gained four pounds. I was surprised but not shocked.

I was terrified to meet with my surgeon after seeing the scale. I knew he was going to be disappointed. But he took it a step further and said my surgery was cancelled. I felt like an absolute failure. How could I throw away the last three months like this? I was in tears and was asking for another chance. It was at this point that I knew I really had a problem. My surgeon gave me two weeks to lose four pounds. I literally went into beast mode. I worked out twice a day, and I drank a shake for breakfast and lunch and had a small dinner. I was told that I would just have to come back in two weeks to verify my weight.

I went back to the office in two weeks to weigh in. Thank God I did it. I had lost six pounds. I felt relieved and sad at the same time that I let food control me in such a way that I almost threw away the whole process. But I decided not to dwell on it and looked forward to the next part of the journey.

Some may think that the worst part was over, but I was about to be tested again. I had to mentally prepare myself for the two-week pre-op diet. My surgeon didn't put me on a full liquid diet, which I was appreciative of; however, I was only able to have a shake for breakfast and lunch and protein and veggies for dinner. To make matters worse, I was celebrating my thirty-ninth birthday during the pre-op process as well as New Year's Eve and New Year's Day. So that meant no going out for dinner, no drinks, no birthday cake.

I struggled hard with this process. It got so bad that I would chew up certain foods and then spit it in the trash can. I remember my surgeon saying to me that if he opened me up the day of surgery and my liver was overly fatty and there was a lot of food in my stomach that he was going to close me up and send me home. When he said that, I wasn't exactly sure if he was joking or not. But I leaned more toward him being very serious. But that still was not enough for me to not sample certain things and then spit them out.

Those thirteen days felt like an eternity. I was going through food withdrawal. I would get unbearable headaches, I felt weak, and I was just overall unhappy. I just chose to stay to myself those two weeks to try and avoid temptation as much as possible. I even had one of my first paying gigs for my business during that time providing training for a high school for five hours. I was so light-headed and weak and even lost my voice that day, but I pushed through.

I made it the thirteen days, and it was finally the day before my surgery. The day before my surgery was a full liquid diet. I could not eat any food and was drinking protein water and spring water the whole day. At that point, I thought I was going to die. I just kept telling myself, "Nicole, you are almost there, why quit today?" And I didn't quit. I was so proud of myself that I made it through this process.

It was finally the day of the surgery, and I was *beyond* nervous. This was my first major surgery. I couldn't get my nerves together at all that day. Thank God my mom was there to sit with me and keep me together. She was back there with me as I was getting prepped for surgery. She is just so amazing. My friend Aqsa met my mom up at the hospital to keep her company that day.

I do not remember much about the surgery. I just remember getting wheeled in the operating room and my surgeon dancing. After that, I was knocked out and woke up in the recovery room. I remember being so high from the anesthesia that I kept falling back asleep. I would wake up in and out of sleep. I remember seeing Aqsa and my mom as I was trying to stay awake. My mom had to leave for a while because she had a meeting for work, so Aqsa stayed and sat with me for a while.

The hospital staff brought me food (if that's what you really want to call it), sugar-free Jell-O, broth, and water. I was sipping water out of little medicine cups. I was eager to get up and walk because I remembered how everyone in my gastric sleeve groups were saying how bad the gas pains could be, so I wanted to make sure that I got up and walked around the hospital floor a couple of times. The pain was not that bad for me. I just felt like I did an insane number of crunches for about a week. Other than that, my pain was very manageable. My blood pressure was very high after surgery, and they had to monitor it all through the night. I was nervous because I was scared that I wasn't going to be released the next day. But I was cleared to go home the next day thankfully.

I stayed at my parents' house for a week during my recovery process. I remember the first day I came home I just slept the whole day away. I didn't realize how much a major surgery takes a toll on you. The pain was a little tough but manageable. And although I saw a psychologist once for this process, I do not think I was mentally prepared for what was to come. Even though I was seeing my therapist regularly, I think we both underestimated how much this surgery would play on my psyche. I went from having an unhealthy relationship with food to having no relationship with food at all. My mind still craved all of the bad food for me, but I knew that it was physically impossible for me to eat any of it. I was on a liquid diet for the first two weeks. Everything caused me such discomfort. I was supposed to try and drink sixty-four ounces of water a day but had no desire to take in any fluids. I was drinking protein shakes all day. All the while I watched everyone around me indulge in all of the things that I used to enjoy eating. It was very hard for me.

I even remember when my family and I went to Jamaica for spring break in April 2019. We got out of the shuttle, and we were being welcomed with beautiful Caribbean cocktails. I wanted one so bad, but I knew it was laden with sugar, and I did not want to be out of the country and experience dumping syndrome. Dumping syndrome is "a medical condition in which your stomach empties its contents into the first part of your small intestine faster than normal. Dumping syndrome is also known as rapid gastric emptying. People with dumping syndrome experience symptoms like nausea and abdominal cramping, diarrhea, cold sweats, weakness, and dizziness." I was terrified of experiencing dumping syndrome. I had read several horror stories of people who experienced this in some of the most inopportune places. Because of this I was always the best patient. I never wanted to experience such a terrible thing. I also remember my aunt who is a nurse telling me about it, and it did nothing but terrified me. And thankfully being over a year out, I never have.

I remember having an emotional breakdown in Jamaica because the sheer fact of being at an all-inclusive resort and not being able to indulge in the endless food and alcoholic drinks just seemed like a complete waste of money to me. As I watched my family drink and eat and truly enjoy the food, I felt left out. I mean, I wasn't crazy enough to think that I expected people to go on this journey with me. But to be on vacation and have to be so regimented absolutely sucked. I remember one night while in Jamaica going back to my room and crying. I did not realize how much I let food control my life. Here I was in beautiful Jamaica, and I was having a breakdown because of food. I promised myself that I was not going to let this ruin my trip. But I knew that this was something that had to be addressed with my therapist when I got back home.

My therapist and I began analyzing my relationship with food. I had this false notion that I could not be happy now that my unhealthy relationship with food was gone. I just felt like I didn't have time to adjust to this drastic change. My therapist suggested that I needed to mourn the death of my food addiction. This seemed silly to me at first, but the more I thought about it, it made perfect sense. It was almost like I experienced a death. I went through all of the stages of grief mourning my relationship with food. I denied the fact that I ever had a negative relationship with food, and I denied the fact that I would never be able to indulge in food the way I used to. I would get angry because food was no longer my safe zone, sad that I could not indulge like others and oftentimes regretful that I even got weight-loss surgery. I would bargain with myself like, "Maybe If I chew this and spit it out, it won't be that bad." I was sad and depressed that I was not able to enjoy certain events with my friends. Happy hours weren't the same. I was tired of hearing how I was not fun to eat with anymore.

Finally, I got to the stage of acceptance. I accepted the fact that I was healthier, and my quality of life improved immensely. I was no longer on blood pressure medication, I no longer had sleep apnea and was off of my CPAP machine, and I lost over one hundred pounds. And most importantly, my confidence skyrocketed, and happiness radiated off of me. My skin was looking amazing; the dark spots on my face cleared up immensely. I was a much healthier version of myself.

But even after the acceptance phase, I still struggled. I loved the support from my sleeve groups because they talked about how real body dysmorphia is. I did and sometimes still do see myself as that 340-pound woman. No matter how many times someone says I look amazing or I have lost a lot of weight, I still do not always see it. To this day, it takes pictures to remind me of how much weight I lost. I still default to going to plus-size websites when shopping for clothes. When I go in stores, I am quick to go to the plus-size section, still thinking that I need a 2x–3x in tops and size eighteen bottoms. I am guessing that this is going to take a while to get used to, although it is not as bad as it used to be. I am still a work in progress in terms of letting my brain catch up with what the mirror and pictures are actually presenting.

CHAPTER 6

Facing the Facts

Our lives improve only when we take chances and the first and most difficult risk we can take is to be honest with ourselves.
—Walter Anderson

So there I stood totally broken. Not knowing where to turn next. All I knew was that I needed to do something, and I needed to do something quick. I was losing my will to fight, my will to live, and my will to go on. I just remember one day I got in my car, got on the Atlantic City Expressway, and started driving. I had no destination in mind, I just drove while blasting my gospel playlist because at that point, I knew it was going to take something supernatural to keep me here on this earth. I cried like I never cried before. I was wailing, and I was scaring myself. I cried so hard that I was making myself sick to the point where I had to pull over.

I was left to face the facts that I and I alone got me here to this point. Because I never believed in myself enough, never loved myself enough, never saw the value in myself enough to know that I deserved more. I never recognized how my lack of self-worth was destroying me until this moment. How did I get here? What conditioned me to make me not only think but believe that I wasn't deserving of happiness or my heart's desires? How, at thirty-eight years old, did I not even know myself?

I had to sit in my truth and realize that a lot of the things that happened in my life I was solely responsible for. Things that I was ashamed of and I wished that I could take back but, unfortunately, I couldn't. And all of that pain, stress, embarrassment, and resentment was a heavy burden on my heart and shoulders. And although I couldn't change my past, I knew that I had to change the present in order to brighten my future.

For as long as I can remember, I put everyone and everything before me. And when I say everything, I mean everything, from family to friends, men/relationships, job, and daughter. Everyone else's happiness came before mine. I would deny what I wanted all the time just to keep the peace. I never wanted to make waves, or I never wanted anyone to be upset with me, so I would often go along with things even if it was totally opposite of what I wanted.

It was time to face the harsh reality that I picked these men because I thought I couldn't do any better. I had to face the harsh reality that I constantly sold myself short in my career or shrunk myself because I didn't want people to be intimidated of me. I had to own that I created this life of mine. And although facing this harsh reality sucked beyond belief, there was just a small piece of me that knew that this was the beginning. The beginning of a journey that would change my life forever. But I could not have prepared myself for how tough this journey was going to be. They say anything worth having is worth fighting for. But my God, I didn't know how hard I would have to fight to save my life.

There I was, ready to begin the work. I called my therapist and told her that I needed to see her that week. And it wasn't my scheduled appointment time because at that point in my life, I was going every other week. It was that moment on the side of the road that I realized I was going to have to put some major work in, and that would begin with me going to therapy every week. I knew that I needed intensive treatment in order to recover and dig myself out of this deep abyss that I had fallen into.

I met with my therapist that next week, and I just remember as soon as my butt hit the chair, I just started sobbing. I couldn't put into words the level of pain I was feeling. All I knew was that I didn't want to be there anymore. And even in the moment of complete and utter despair, I was thinking in my head about everyone but myself. What would my parents think if they knew I was contemplating suicide and had to be committed? What would my brothers think? What if people found out that I was not as strong as they thought I was? Would my friends want to be friends with someone who was mentally unstable like me? How did I get this bad? How did I value the opinions of everyone else over my own? These were all the questions that I needed to find answers to in order to grow.

I had to accept and reassure myself that everything that I went through in my life happened for a reason. All of the burdens, pain, and depression I faced wasn't accidental. I was looking at it all wrong. I was looking at it as if I were the victim and everyone wronged me. But I go back to what I said earlier. Everything we experience in life, no matter how painful, we either invite it, accept it, or allow it. I had to face the fact that I allowed the cheating in my relationships to continue because I did not walk away. I accepted the fact that I had no legal rights in my daughter's life, so I allowed him to control me through her. I invited men to not value me because I ultimately did not value myself. These cold, hard facts were tough to accept.

I remember when I was in a session with my first therapist and she said to me that men "can sense the desperation" I gave off. When I tell you that I was so enraged when she said this to me, I grappled with myself back and forth on whether I was even going to include this in this book. I was mad, I was hurt, I was embarrassed, and I was ashamed. And I did not want anyone to know how bad I really was when it came to men. But I also recognize for healing to truly happen, I have to stand in my truth no matter how ugly it is. And just because that was my reality at that time did not mean that it was going to be like that forever. Despite my past, I am still capable of achieving great things in my life, but first I had to accept my past and build on it.

Although me accepting myself and my reality absolutely scared the shit out of me, I knew that it had to happen. I had to practice radical honesty with myself. The radical honesty in my case was how can I truly love myself when I did not even know who the real me was? My therapist would tell me repeatedly that true self-love is the most healing task that I can master. Working through the changes in my thinking, my responses, my outlook, and attitude about people would be life changing. And although I hung on her every word, that task just seemed too daunting. But again, all of my self-doubt, lack of self-worth and love, and self-defensiveness drove me right to a deep depression.

Even though it felt damn near impossible to change, I knew I had no other choice. I chose to face the facts. I was ready to admit all of my shortcomings and, most importantly, ask myself for forgiveness. I knew there were probably a few people I needed to ask for their forgiveness. I knew that it was more important to forgive myself. Forgive myself for not recognizing my greatness, forgive myself for repeatedly accepting less than I deserve, forgive myself for not loving myself, and forgive myself for being my own worst enemy.

Something that I was always guilty of was constructing a persona that I would constantly tell myself that others would find more likable or respectable than I really was. But a persona that I constructed was not real. It was indeed unnatural. But I felt like if I would deny my wants, dreams, and desires to keep the peace, then that would make me more likable. And although people might have liked me more because I was always agreeable, I was miserable. And to take it a step further, anytime I would be around someone who was comfortable in their own skin, I would pick them apart in my head and try to find flaws within them. How sad is that? Someone who loves themselves made me truly uncomfortable. The fact that they were at peace with themselves would make me angry and jealous at the same time.

Standing in my truth was not going to be easy. I knew that I was going to have to evaluate my current situation, accept my current reality, and work beyond hard to remain true to myself. I knew that I was going to have to make life-changing decisions in order to live the life I ultimately wanted. I knew that this might include ending a relationship so that I could gain back my life and self-confidence, end friendships that were no longer serving me or even derailing me, and leave a job that was draining me physically, mentally, and emotionally.

Being honest with myself wasn't easy, and it did not happen overnight. I knew that this process was going to require a lot of patience, dedication, willpower, and sacrifice. But I kept telling myself that the short- and long-term benefits would far outweigh the sacrifice. These next chapters will lay out my spiritual awakening, my healing, and ultimately, my process to self-love.

CHAPTER 7

Botched Beliefs

If you accept a limited belief, then it will
become a truth for you.
—Louise Hay

Have you ever taken the time out to think if *you* could be the one holding yourself back from achieving success or *you* could possibly be limiting your results because of what *you* believe?

One thing that I learned about myself while I was and continue to be on this journey of self-actualization is that my botched way of thinking has hindered me in every aspect of my life. My skewed thinking, more formally known as self-limiting beliefs, is something, believe it or not, we all struggle with. However, my self-limiting beliefs were crippling.

Self-limiting beliefs refers to "assumptions or perceptions that you've got about yourself and about the way the world works. These assumptions are self-limiting because in some way they're holding you back from achieving what you are capable of." And here is the thing about self-limiting beliefs: no matter how bad you say you want something, if you believe that it is unattainable or for some reason you do not deserve it, one of two things will happen: either you will not let yourself have it, or you will allow yourself to have it, but you will always believe that you do not deserve it and will ultimately fuck it up. I know, sounds harsh, doesn't it? But in every aspect of my life where I had a self-limiting belief tied to it, that is what ultimately happened.

Limiting beliefs can come from many places including parents, teachers, coaches, media, society, and culture. They are formed by repetitive thoughts and are mostly created in childhood by repeated interactions with those around us. A lot of our self-limiting beliefs are passed down from generation to generation. So oftentimes we are carrying around beliefs that are not even our own. We just believe them because, well, that's how we were raised.

For example, I was always told that if I didn't go to college, I wouldn't get a good job or have money. Growing up, I was always told that going to college was mandatory. So I went to college, majored in social work, moved back to NJ, and got my first full-time job making $28,000 a year. Now although this was back in 2003, there was still no way that I could afford to live on my own in NJ. I lived with my parents during this time. I also grew up with the self-limiting belief that going to school for a skilled trade was not good enough. When I wanted to go to the vocational high school in my area instead of my traditional high school, my parents told me no because that school was for kids who were not going to college. And that stuck with me for a long time.

So how did this self-limiting belief manifest itself in my adult life? I frowned upon any man that tried to talk to me if he did not go to college or ultimately had a skilled trade and/or dirty job, which translated to having no money, and would ultimately not be able to support me. See how skewed this way of thinking was? As I look back on all the good men I might have missed out on because I immediately dismissed them because of their jobs, it's kind of saddening.

Now this is just the tip of the iceberg for me. This was just one small example of the self-limiting beliefs I had. Several other limiting beliefs I had included:

- I am too old to have kids.
- I am successful at everything except weight loss.
- Trusting someone (more so a man) is too hard.
- I will never experience true love.
- I am not beautiful because I am overweight.
- Comfort food helps me feel better.

These botched beliefs have kept me from all of the things that I truly wanted in life. This is when the true work started in therapy. My therapist would have me take each limiting belief one by one and made me assign a percentage regarding how much I believed this limiting belief to be true. I will let you know how much I truly believed each one of these self-limiting beliefs.

- I am too old to have kids—80 percent
- I am successful at everything except weight loss—70 percent
- Trusting someone (more so a man) is too hard—100 percent
- I will never experience true love—95 percent
- I am not beautiful because I am overweight—90 percent
- Comfort food helps me feel better—80 percent

My results were staggering. I believed all of these things at such alarming rates. And in all of my years, I never once took the time to discover why all of these things continued to manifest themselves in my life. I was in no way prepared for the amount of work that it was going to take to unlearn every single one of them.

The first step was to take each self-limiting belief and say whether it was true or false. Saying that I will never experience true love is false. Just because I have not found my soul mate yet does not mean that it is *never* going to happen. And if that is the case, how can this belief be true?

Then there is the self-limiting belief that I am too old to have kids. Some women are waiting until they are older in life to have children. Hell, even Janet Jackson had her baby when she was fifty. Kenya Moore from *Real Housewives of Atlanta* had her baby after age forty-five. With that said, what makes me think that I am too old to have a baby?

Another self-limiting belief I carried with me for years is that I am successful at everything except weight loss. Now, one would think from my weight woes chapter that this might be true. But even after I lost over 100 pounds, I was still saying and believing I was not successful at weight loss. How can that be true? Well, the fact that I did not make the goal weight that my surgeon set for me or the goal that I set for myself meant I still considered myself a failure. Never mind the fact that I have lost 103 pounds. I was disappointed in myself because I did not lose the last 38 pounds according to my surgeon and the last 18 pounds for the goal weight I set for myself. The bottom line is I am successful at weight loss because I lost 103 pounds. But subconsciously I have been carrying this botched belief for so long it has stalled my weight loss because what we think, believe, and say is what we will manifest.

The next self-limiting belief I carried was that trusting someone is too hard. And although with this belief I preface it by saying "someone," the truth of the matter is the belief only pertained to men. I am more than able to trust my female friends and even male friends who are strictly platonic friends. But when it comes down to being in relationships, I believed that trusting a man was too hard. All of my relationships ended in lies and deceit, including my relationship with my college sweetheart. Even though I was only twenty-one years old, I loved that man. I am still not sure that I have experienced the chemistry we shared again to date. And all I know is this was the first time that I was ever lied to by a man. And I also believe that this is when this self-limiting belief was established. Ever since that relationship, I believed that it was too hard to trust a man I was in a relationship with. Because I was carrying this belief, what do you think happened? Every relationship I have been in has been with someone I couldn't trust. There has not been one relationship that I have been in that I felt secure. To take that a step further, my intuition always told me when something wasn't right. However, I would never listen, which in the end cost me dearly in every single relationship. The real truth behind this belief is that I did not find it hard to trust someone. The harsh reality was I can trust, I just needed to work hard on trusting myself.

The last crippling belief I had was that comfort food makes me feel better. This is one that I have carried the majority of my life. Being overweight as a kid, I remember eating chips, sweets, candy, and other unhealthy things when I was sad. I always believed that it was the comfort food that would make me feel better. I used food as therapy to make me feel better. And as I got older, it just got worse. A bad day at work, I was going to happy hour for drinks and appetizers. A bad breakup, I was ordering food every day or eating all of the unhealthy snacks in my pantry. Feeling depressed, I was stuck on the couch drinking and eating the most savory, greasy foods. And in my subconscious, I truly believed that all the terrible food I ate was what made me feel better.

But I know this not to be true because every time I would eat these things was because of some negative emotion I was feeling. I always felt terrible afterward. I would feel like a glutton for overindulging. My stomach would hurt, and I would feel stuffed to the point that I could vomit. In reality, it did not make me feel better at all. I would feel like a fat ass who could not control herself, which in turn would make me feel even worse. This self-limiting belief hurt me in more ways than one. This is how I ended up over 340 pounds. This is how I built such an unhealthy relationship with food.

We all have core beliefs that guide the decisions we make on a daily basis. These core beliefs affect how we interpret events in our lives, and they influence the way we think, feel, and behave. Our healthy beliefs are the ones that serve us well. However, it is the self-limiting beliefs that keep us from achieving our greatest potential. I am not the only person that suffers from crippling self-limiting beliefs. But because these limiting beliefs operate in the subconscious mind, we don't really pay attention to them—all the while they are tearing us apart piece by piece.

There are essentially three types of self-limiting beliefs that can keep you from being the best version of yourself. They are: unhealthy beliefs about yourself, unhealthy beliefs about others, and unhealthy beliefs about the world. Unhealthy beliefs lead to unhealthy habits, and these unhealthy habits create negative consequences that ultimately reinforce the unhealthy beliefs. This creates a repetitive, malicious cycle that becomes very challenging to break.

But the great news is that it isn't impossible. I want to share how I broke out of these self-limiting beliefs in hopes of helping you do the same. And the scariest things about self-limiting beliefs is most of us think we don't have them, and they are hard to spot. I had never heard about a self-limiting belief until my therapist introduced this to me.

First, I had to recognize and own that my self-limiting beliefs ultimately turned into self-fulfilling prophecies. For example, I believed that I would never experience true love, which ultimately meant that I felt I was unlovable. And as a result, I jumped from one unhealthy relationship to the next over and over again. All the men that I was in relationships with treated me poorly, which reinforced my belief that I would never find true love or that I was unlovable.

Another example of how my self-limiting beliefs turned into a self-fulfilling prophecy was my belief that trusting someone was too hard. Even when people were nice to me, I assumed that they were lying or they had ulterior motives. If someone told me that I was beautiful, I would think they were lying to me or were just trying to get me in bed.

There was one time when I posted a picture on Facebook when I was in Florida for my friend Trinetta's fortieth birthday dinner. I was being hard on myself as I was getting dressed, complaining that my shaper was not holding my stomach in enough and my arms were looking huge. But when my friend Trinetta took the picture and showed it to me, I was in total shock. I looked *amazing*. It was at that moment in October 2019 that I actually *believed* it for myself. Trinetta told me that I should post the picture, so I did. So many people were commenting how great I looked, but for some reason, I didn't believe the majority of people that commented. I was telling myself, "Well, it's probably because I do not post on social media often that people are commenting."

I was telling my new therapist about it at my next session. He asked me how many commented on the photo, and I responded with about sixty. His question to me was, "So you mean to tell me all sixty people were lying to you?" and I emphatically said yes. But again, this self-limiting belief was now a self-fulfilling prophecy. Because I believed that it was too hard to trust someone, that meant that I believed everyone was inherently untrustworthy. As a result, I kept everyone at a distance and never developed trusting relationships—more specifically with men. And any time that I was lied to, cheated on, or felt like I wasn't treated fairly, I believed that this was evidence to further prove my self-limiting belief that people are untrustworthy.

How do you change your self-limiting beliefs? I will not lie to you and say that it will be easy. Reason being many of these unhealthy beliefs are ones we have carried for several years and for the most part believe that they are 100 percent true. Furthermore, we spend our lives looking for evidence that reinforces these negative beliefs, all the while ignoring evidence to the contrary at the same damn time.

How does one start to unlearn these beliefs that have been crippling them for years? Identifying and acknowledging your self-limiting beliefs is the first step in taking back your own power. The only way to truly eliminate these self-limiting beliefs is to make the conscious choice to work on your own belief system. You have to weed out any beliefs that aren't serving your greater good or limiting you in any way. With that said, you are not going to talk yourself out of self-limiting beliefs overnight. Remember, these are the negative thoughts that you have told yourself day in and day out both consciously and subconsciously. Telling yourself that you are not worthless will not suddenly make you believe that you are worthy deep down inside. The most successful way to change your beliefs is to challenge your beliefs head-on. To do that, I had to abandon all of the negative thoughts that were draining my mental strength. By abandoning my habits, I was able to slowly chip away at my self-limiting beliefs one piece at a time.

In order to eliminate my self-limiting beliefs, I started saying each one out loud, and I would ask myself, "Do I know this to be true?" Every time I was in therapy and I discussed my limiting beliefs with my therapist, he always asked me, "Has it been validated?" meaning, "Have I experienced these enough times for it to be true?" It is very difficult to draw accurate conclusions from a small number of experiences. Once I was able to prove that a belief was not validated or simply untrue, I would develop a new belief that would positively serve me. The key was to create a belief that would improve my life and support my ability to take action to make my life better. Some of the new beliefs that I created for myself were:

- I am beautiful at any size.
- I love my height, my complexion, my curves.
- I am an amazing woman with a sound mind.
- I am a better woman today than I was yesterday.
- I am worthy.
- I am in charge of my happiness.

These are just a few of the new beliefs that I created for myself.

If I leave you with one thing, please remember that you have to continue examining your life for limiting beliefs and eliminating them. Eliminating our self-limiting beliefs can be just like pulling weeds: no matter how much you try to pull the weed from the root, some weeds will resurface. If they happen to re-surface, recognize it, and then eliminate it.

CHAPTER 8

Reaching for Redemption

No human being is so bad as to be beyond redemption.
—Mahatma Gandhi

What is redemption? Redemption means, in the context of your life, "returning to your natural self, returning to your deeper awareness, and, if you are a believer, returning to your connection with God and what God has sent you into the world to do." Redemption means taking something bad and turning it into something good. When achieved, redemption can reestablish your connection with the deeper knowledge placed within you— to guide you and to protect you and to lead you to a greater life, a greater life that you have not yet discovered.

Whether you think you need it or not, at some point in our lives, redemption will be necessary in some shape, form, or fashion. When the idea of redemption surfaces, it's usually because of some sort of painful choice we made. This choice and, in my case series of choices, left my previously well-polished character and reputation suddenly marred by guilt, embarrassment, and shame. It left me totally in despair and without hope.

The funny thing about redemption is that it is not a fictional idea. Redemption actually exists. What makes it very difficult to achieve is that it can't be given to you.

When most people think of redemption, it may be along the lines of someone committing a heinous crime and then seeking redemption for their wrongdoings. For example, someone who murdered someone may seek redemption and forgiveness from those whom this heinous crime affected. Or someone who stole millions of dollars from unsuspecting people may at some point in their life seek redemption. However, for me it was different. And although there may have been someone that I may need to seek redemption from, I was more so seeking redemption for myself.

The path to redemption is difficult but not impossible. And in order for true redemption to occur, you must fully recognize that you've done wrong, accept responsibility of having done it, and vow to never do it again; apologize to those you've done it to; and finally commit to improving yourself. In my case, I struggled with redemption for a whole year. I would see my therapist week after week and beat myself up for being so dumb, for giving people power over my life, for not loving myself enough to know that I deserved more, for accepting less than I deserved for far too long, and for not seeing the beautiful woman that stood before me.

The thing is with me, I never needed anyone to be critical of me. I was always hard on myself. In a way, it was a coping mechanism for me. I did not need anyone to be critical of me because I would take care of that myself. It was almost like "let me beat myself up before anyone else has a chance to." In my mind, I thought that this was helping me. But in the end, all this did was tear down the very person whom I wanted to uplift the most. How do I go about forgiving myself when I felt like I was the most gullible, dumbest smart person I ever met in my life?

I used to often ask myself, "Why me? Why did God pick me to experience hardship after hardship? What about me made anyone think that I was strong enough to handle all of this heartache?" I could not answer these questions at first. But as I moved through the stages of seeking redemption, I learned, "Why not me?" Because what I went through was one of the most valuable experiences in my life. They didn't teach what I went through in my doctoral program. I can't earn a doctorate degree in "growing up not loving myself." The only way someone can learn what it's like to lack self-worth and self-love to the point that it is self-destructive yet still come out on the other side is to live through it. And that is exactly what happened to me. No matter how much someone told me it is important to love yourself first or no one is going to love me more than me, I would have never known how truly damaging it is when you do not love yourself if I did not experience it for myself. And as a result, I am able to share my testimony in hopes of being able to help people going through the same thing. If I am able to help just one person, then I know my struggle was not in vain.

How did I achieve redemption? I will lay out the steps mentioned above in more detail. When I decided to face the facts outlined in the previous chapter, I knew that's when I fully recognized that I had done myself wrong for far too many years. Any time that I looked in the mirror and said unkind things to myself, I was doing wrong. Anytime that I allowed someone to constantly disrespect me, I was doing myself wrong because, ultimately,

I didn't respect myself. In continuing to work at a place that did not value my skills, aptitude, and experience, I was doing myself wrong. So now that I recognized all of these things, I knew I was able to take on the next step of redemption.

Accepting responsibility was very hard for me at first. In the beginning of my redemption journey, I blamed *everyone* except myself. I was that person that could've stood on a mountain top and yelled, "I AM A VICTIM." I pretended for a long time that people in my life wronged me and how could they do that to someone who is so loving, kind, and caring. This is what I believed for the longest time.

I remember one session my first therapist saying to me, "You are not a victim, Nicole." One thing I would always notice in therapy, when something she said made me uncomfortable or challenged me in a way that I was not ready or willing to accept at the time, it would make me angry. When she said that to me, in my mind, I was like, "How dare she?" But the more we processed it, the more I realized she was absolutely right. I was not a victim. I was not raped, I was not robbed at gunpoint, I was not a child that was physically abused, I was not murdered, so how dare I try to say that I was a victim? The true definition of a victim is "a person harmed, injured, or killed as a result of a crime, accident, or other event or action." This was a very defining moment for me. It was at this point that I was able to accept responsibility.

I had to accept responsibility for the fact that everything I went through was on me. It is a true fact that people can only do what you allow them to do. I had to accept the fact that my desperation of wanting to be in a relationship so bad made me overlook glaring red flags in all of my relationships. I had to accept the fact that my desire to experience motherhood so bad made me stay in a loveless relationship way too long. I had to accept the fact that because I didn't think I was beautiful because I was overweight that it caused me to "date down" because I felt like people on my level would not find me attractive.

I was at a place where I accepted responsibility, and I vowed to never do it again. But was it just that easy? I knew that when it came to dating, I had to take a major break from it all. After my relationship with Hassan, I took out time for myself. I was single for over two years. Now, don't get me wrong, I did entertain a date here and there, but it was nothing serious. I knew that I needed to take time to get to know me and what I really wanted out of life in order to keep from making the same mistakes over and over. This was critical to my healing. Oftentimes we do not want to take the time to ultimately heal from what is ailing us. We try to mend a broken heart by finding distractions, hoping that someone new will help us forget the old. However, all we do is take that baggage into the new situation, and our wounds that are still open tend to bleed on the new person. I knew that I did not want to become that cynical woman that subscribed to the "all men ain't shit" mentality.

Taking time for myself was a huge struggle for me. I did not know how to not be with anyone. And although I was always in a relationship, I was still always lonely. This was something else that I had to take responsibility for. Another one of my self-limiting beliefs was "If I do not have a man, I am lonely." The mere fact that when I was in a relationship I still felt lonely should have been enough to debunk that negative belief, but it wasn't. I had to create a new narrative that would totally change my way of thinking. My therapist made me define the difference of being lonely and being alone. In its simplest terms, being alone means being by myself.

However, being lonely is more of an emotional response. A person is lonely when they feel abandoned or sad due to isolation. The truth was that I felt that I was unworthy of attention or regard from others. So that was my self-fulfilling prophecy.

I had to apologize to myself for feeling like this, and I committed to improving on this. The reality was that I can be alone and still be very happy. I finally understood that I am good enough by myself. I am a valuable person, and I do not need the approval of anyone else for this to be true. When I am alone, I constantly remind myself that it's because I choose to be. Being alone really is a choice. The more that I embraced that, the more I recognized that it is very easy to find someone to spend time with, but when I elevated my standards for the people I allowed into my life, I was telling myself that I am better off by myself than with someone who isn't a great fit for me.

I also learned to value my own opinion more. In the past, when faced with a difficult decision, I would solicit the advice of those closest to me. In hindsight, I depended on others to decide for me because I did not trust myself. As I continued on my path to redemption, I learned that it is OK to value another person's opinion, but I must value my own more. The more time that I spent asking myself for advice, the less I started to need input from others. When I began to trust myself to solve problems, I became a much stronger and more confident woman, and that allowed me to face challenges head-on that I wouldn't have felt capable of before.

I also learned to appreciate silence more. I used these opportunities to find out what it feels like to enjoy my own company. I found my love of reading again, I started journaling more, I even started practicing meditation (although I still have not mastered that). I started praying more, I started finding positive affirmations that I could say to myself in the morning when I wake up before I turn on the TV or look at my phone, and when work would start stressing me out, I would use my lunch break to walk around campus. The world is a busy place, and unless we take the time to take a breath and step away from it every once in a while, it's easy to forget how beautiful it is to be alone and enjoy your own company. I have learned so much about myself in the moments when I am least occupied, the times when there is nothing to distract me from my thoughts and feelings. The things I learned about myself did not always make me smile, but they did help me grow.

Learning to be OK with being alone also taught me how to speak kindly to myself. We all have an inner voice. "An internal monologue, also called self-talk, *inner* speech, *inner* discourse or internal discourse, is a person's *inner voice* which provides a running verbal monologue of thoughts while they are conscious." ("Self-Talk.") Our inner voice is usually tied to our sense of self. We all have an inner voice that talks to us all hours of the day, whether it is while you are in the shower, driving to work, watching TV, etc. Sometimes you do not even recognize when your inner voice is talking to you.

For the longest time, my inner voice was so mean spirited and negative. As a result, I had my conscious and subconscious mind being mean to me. This is why I knew it was critical during my time alone to get to know my inner voice and learn how to talk to it. I realized that by always being in the company of others that it was easier to ignore my inner voice, but when I am alone, it's just me. And this inner voice had more power over me than anyone else ever could. The way that I talked to myself when no one was around shaped me into who I am more than anything else.

I knew at this point that I had to completely distance myself from my negative inner voice. A book that was very instrumental in helping me eliminate my negative inner voice was *The Power of Now* by Eckhart Tolle. Tolle's core message is that people's emotional problems are rooted in their identification with their minds. Tolle helped me to be aware of my "present moment" instead of losing myself in worry and anxiety about the past or future. This book was life changing for me. This was one of the many books that my therapist recommended to me.

Working on healing my negative inner voice allowed me to become my own best friend. I started thinking to myself what I would say to my best friend if they came to me with those same negative thoughts, and then I applied those answers to myself. I would take the time to ask myself if the negative thoughts I had been saying to myself were serving me in a positive way. Is it helping me to become the best version of myself or holding me back? Whenever I would fall back into the negative inner voice, I would go back to these steps.

Interestingly enough, the final step in my redemption phase was my conscious affirmation to become a woman who would strive only to do good even knowing that I would fall short at times. This ultimately equipped me to forgive myself and find redemption in my heart for myself. Every day when I wake up, I say to myself, "I will be a better woman than I was yesterday. And for me that is attainable. Because I am running my own race. I am in competition with no one." As long as you strive to be a better representation of yourself on a daily basis, it takes away the pressure of trying to be perfect, which ultimately does not exist.

CHAPTER 9

Soul Searching

Some changes look negative on the surface but you will
soon realize that space is being created in your life for
something new to emerge.
—Eckhart Tolle

Have you ever had a moment where you woke up and things just felt different? You just felt different? This was a defining moment for me, and although I know that miraculously I just didn't wake up one day and all of a sudden I was a changed woman, but that day my awakening truly manifested itself. It was at that moment that I knew my life would be forever changed. And it is one of those things that once it finally happens, you will never be able to return to the old version of yourself.

I have always considered myself to be a religious person. I was raised in a Baptist church as a kid. My paternal grandfather was a deacon at the church I attended as a child. I was in the children's choir, I attended Sunday school, and I was baptized at this same church. I just always went to church, listened to the sermon, and went home. Once I went away to college, I stopped going to church. I would go with my girlfriend Trinetta from time to time, but I did not go consistently.

It was not until I became a mother that I started going back to church regularly. It had become a tradition for me, my mom, and my daughter to go every Sunday. We would go to early service and then go to breakfast afterward. It created such great memories for me, my mom, and my daughter.

However, one day I just stopped going. There was nothing in particular that happened. I just stopped. I even remember my daughter asking me one day why we stopped going to church, and that made me feel terrible. My excuse for not going to my childhood church anymore was that it was too far. I lived about forty-five minutes from my church home, and getting to the eight a.m. early service was like getting up early for work. I started visiting churches in my area, but none of them felt like home. And then when I started going through my storm in 2017, I just stopped going altogether. I stopped praying, and I even started questioning God. I would question why he would want me to go through all of this pain. There would be days where I would fall down to my knees and sob and pray to God. There were also times where I would be lying in my bed and I would talk to God too. But this was nothing that I would do consistently.

When I was going through my storm, people would tell me that I would have to have blind faith and trust in God that he would make a way. But to be totally honest, my faith had diminished. And it waned to the point that I did not think things were going to work out in my favor. The only thing that remained constant for me was my love of gospel music. Even in my darkest moments, I could play some of my go-to songs, and I would instantly start to feel better, if even for a moment. I would blast these songs as loud as my volume would go, lift my hands in the air, and sing. I would then get this overwhelming chill over my body and get goose bumps at the same time. I would catch myself having this tingly sensation running through my body. I knew that all was not lost with me and my belief in God.

But I was yearning for more. I felt that there was still something missing from my life. At the time, I did not know what it was. But I was willing to dig deeper to find out what it was.

I oftentimes found myself asking questions that were on a deeper level. I began to question my old beliefs, habits, and social conditioning. I was also beginning to see that there is so much more to life than what I had been taught. There was so much more to life than my self-limiting beliefs. There was so much more than the social constructs I lived by all of my life. I was determined to dig deeper.

I spent a year in this space, and at the time, I didn't know what it was. As I continued to do some deep soul searching with the help of my therapist, it finally clicked. I was having a spiritual awakening. And all I know is that it was one of the most confusing, lonely, alienating, yet extremely beautiful experiences in my life. Everything that I once believed and held on to as true changed. The things that I once thought brought me happiness didn't matter anymore. Up until the age of thirty-nine, I was going through life pursuing the emptiness of money, relationships, power, a high-power career, and respect in an attempt to find "happiness." Chasing all of these things never made me happy. In actuality, chasing these things made me even sadder.

I found myself asking questions on a much deeper level such as "Who am I? What is my purpose in my life? Why am I here? Why did God choose me to suffer the way he did?" These were soul-stirring questions that were questions that could not be answered in one day. These have been questions that I always wanted answers to but was too terrified to touch because sometimes it is so much easier to live in oblivion. I knew that once I actually began to soul search and genuinely find the answers to these questions, it was going to be painful.

The process with my spiritual awakening started with me questioning the basic foundation of Christianity. My father, who has been an avid researcher for years of African history, was the one who made me start questioning the things that I was taught. I was beginning to question and doubt some of my early teachings of the Bible, and I was beginning to sense that there was so much more to life than what the Bible and Christianity declared. And I wanted to learn more. My dad helped me out a lot through this process by sharing a wealth of knowledge with me. I used the information that my dad gathered for me and got to work. The research that my dad provided had me questioning all of my former beliefs, desires, and paradigms. Many of them I challenged, and some of them were even disproven. This was completely soul stirring and traumatic but completely necessary for this spiritual awakening.

As I was working on myself and soul searching, I had no earthly idea what was going on inside of me. I felt like I couldn't talk to anyone about it either because I had no idea of how to explain it or put it into words. It created a very lonely season for me because this was something that I had to do alone. And although this time brought me so much clarity in terms of my purpose in life, it also brought unexplainable pain right along with it.

The more soul searching I did, the more connected I felt to my soul. I could literally feel my soul evolving, expanding, and maturing. It was like an invisible weight that I had been carrying on my chest for years was slowly disappearing. Each day my heart was not as heavy. I could actually breathe. And not in the natural sense but in the spiritual sense. It is just something that can't be explained, only experienced. My connection to my soul continued to grow, and I was loving the transformation as a result. All of the negative emotions I would feel on a daily basis were being replaced with positive ones. I was feeling unspeakable joy, peace, freedom, and self-love. My heart was full. Full of all of the things I once looked at external factors to provide. I as I stood was simply enough.

In an effort to be as totally transparent as possible, I am sharing something that I wrote in preparation for one of my sessions entitled "My Journey" in November 2018. This is my spiritual awakening:

MY JOURNEY

A journey: "A process of reconciliation and learning through enlightenment." I would describe my journey as more of a spiritual awakening. I am becoming more conscious and aware of events, actions, practices that have lasted too long that must change. Taking my life back into my own hands and escaping the bondage that was imposed on me through society in order to really know happiness and live the life I truly want to live—which is a life not dictated by television, people, magazines, movies, social identifications, etc. As my consciousness grows, my interest evolves, the meaning of life changes for me, and I have new aspirations and inspirations.

My journey has included:

Feeling that something has changed inside of me, I have escaped from my comfort zone, which at times scares me, as sometimes it feels easier to just go back to what is easy. But knowing that this is just an illusion and that I have finally dropped the mask and that my blinders are gone, I feel as if I can see everything much clearer.

Awareness of harmful habits—I realize all the things I used to do that were harmful to my peace, and I don't want to do them anymore, all of the limiting beliefs and thinking patterns that I wish to eliminate.

Not feeling good with my old circle of friends and feeling the need to be alone or with new people—Learning that not everyone around me evolves at the same speed. Not feeling guilty for not wanting to be around certain people and recognizing that some friendships are only here for a season. No longer trying to force friendships that have expired. Recognizing that the gap between us has become too big. I began to look for people more in alignment with who I really am and my new energy. Finding genuine friendships in the most profound form, but yet it is an energy I never felt before.

A deep yearning for meaning in my life—A lot of things that I used to do before are of no interest to me anymore (excessive drinking, overindulging in food, gossiping, partying). I have a profound interest in doing things that are authentic.

Hypersensitivity—My spiritual senses have increased—my conscious has kicked into full gear, I am extremely inspired now to continue to build my passion (being a black-owned business owner, author, influencer), my emotions are more in check.

Willingness to know who I truly am—I do not want to be defined by society or others anymore. I am tired of wearing the mask I have been wearing for too long in order to be what others expected of me. I am fearfully and wonderfully made. I love the woman who stares back at me.

Loss of interest in all forms of conflict—My inner peace is sacred. Conflict has started to make me feel uncomfortable, as I am able to feel energy shifts in my body. My friends' dramas don't interest me anymore, me talking about people doesn't interest me. I want inner peace and deep serenity. With that has come a lost in interest in "being right."

Loss of interest in judging others but most importantly myself—I want to bring more peace, love, compassion for others and in my life. I want to celebrate myself for the amazing person that I am. I want to see the beauty in me every day and see myself from a place of love.

With that said, you never fully arrive at the end of your journey/awakening. A journey is nothing more than the process of learning through something. I guess this makes me a lifelong learner of self, and therefore, there is no end to this journey.

The scariest and most gratifying part about a spiritual awakening is that it will happen when you least expect it. You cannot plan for it. It just happens. A spiritual awakening will creep into your life and then shake everything up like a hurricane. And although it will sneak up on you, the hidden gem in all of this is that it will occur at the precise time you need it the most. Thankfully, this was the exact case for me. Right when I was ready to give up on myself, God, and the world, it happened, and I am forever grateful for how this saved my life and changed my life for the better. Deep in my soul, I finally accepted that external factors never have and never will bring me true happiness or fulfillment. There is nothing outside of me that can ever make me feel worthy. I know this for a fact because no matter how many times I was told I was loved or beautiful or amazing, it didn't matter. Because I didn't believe it for myself. Everything that I ever wanted or needed was always within me. I just never valued myself enough to notice. But once I learned to validate myself, what others thought of me began to matter less and less. I encourage anyone who has the opportunity to experience a spiritual awakening to not run from it, no matter how painful it might be. Because sometimes your life and well-being depend on it. And once you embrace this spiritual awakening, there is nothing but a life-changing experience on the other side.

CHAPTER 10

Protecting My Peace

If you cannot find peace within yourself, you will never find it anywhere else.
—Marvin Gaye

Now that I had the opportunity to have a spiritual awakening, I found myself asking, "Now what?" I did not want all that I just experienced to be in vain, so I had to come up with a game plan to make sure that I would stay on the right path. But what would that consist of?

For starters, I felt like my therapist I had for years had taken me as far as I could go. I could never put into words how much she helped me over the years. She saw me at the absolute lowest points of my life, and she helped me through it all. I could never thank her enough. Yet I knew it was time for something different. I started looking for a black male therapist. I felt like totally switching things up with therapy could take me to the pinnacle of my transformation.

I was in a much better place physically, mentally, and emotionally, but I felt like I still had about 15 percent more to go to get to a place of complete healing. I met with my new therapist for the first time, and I will be honest, I wasn't sure at first. I felt like we spent the majority of the initial session looking at each other and him asking questions and me answering questions. But I wasn't getting a good vibe from it. I remember calling my mom on the way home from my first session with him and telling her it was a no go. My mom told me that I shouldn't be so hasty in my decision and I at least needed to give it a solid month before I decided he wasn't the right fit for me.

Because I value my mother's advice, that is exactly what I did. I went to him for four sessions before I made my decision, and I am glad I did. I still continue to see him to this day. He has helped me with not being so hard on myself. His calm spirit and demeanor are exactly what I need as I am learning to protect my peace.

He would often tell me to fake it until I believed it. I didn't always understand what he meant by that. One day I decided to ask him to go into further detail about this concept. He then proceeded to ask me a few probing questions. He asked me how would my life be different if my peace of mind was steady and anchored? How would I live my life if others couldn't control my moods? What would my life look like if I was unbothered by the ruthlessness of the world around me? Those were some pretty heavy questions for me to consider, but I knew that everything he asked me had a purpose.

I knew that if my peace of mind was steady and anchored, then I knew that I would not be moved when my supervisor started micromanaging me and would question my talents or abilities. I would not lash out at her because I would know that her micromanaging said more about her than it did me. I knew that her being a micromanager did not change the fact that I was a doctor, I was an amazing writer, I excelled at developing programs, and that I am a people person. If my peace of mind was steady and anchored, then I would know that there was nothing that could disrupt my peace but me. This really helped me when I was working at the college. The job itself was not hard at all. It was the people. I changed my way of thinking when it came to that job. I was not going to let things that I could not control rattle me. People are going to be who they are. But if I continued to give my power to others by allowing them to get under my skin, then that was on me. That was not protecting my peace.

Another question he asked me was, "How would you live your life if others could not control your moods?" I related that question specifically to dating. If someone treated me unkind or did not recognize my worth, that would not affect my mood at all because how someone treats me says more about them. Just because a man does not recognize my worth does not mean that I am not worthy of love.

I have a perfect example of this. After my dating hiatus, I met someone who I thought was a great guy on paper. I will call him Rob. I met Rob on POF (yes, I know, mistake number one!). I remember seeing this guy on another dating site years ago. I have a great memory when it comes to things like that. I viewed his profile, but I didn't speak because I remembered he was full of shit last time. He sent me a message, so I responded. It probably had something to do with the fact that I was out in Philly celebrating my friend Chris's birthday and I had had way too much to drink that night. We were in the club, and Rob said that he wanted to meet me. I told Chris that I was going to be right back.

I went out to meet him, and we talked for a bit and then decided we would go out on a date the next day.

We ended up dating for six months. And let me just tell you, *everything* about him was a lie, from his age, his jobs, where he went to college (I still never got confirmation if he really went), to where he lived. Simply everything. I mean he would lie about the dumbest stuff. It was quite scary. Now, the old me prior to my spiritual awakening would've carried this relationship on for years until something so devastating happened that I would've had no choice but to leave. And then once I left, I would've beaten myself up something terrible because I was so dumb. But this time it was different. I will not lie and say that I didn't have my day of being sad, but I did not stay there. He chose to be deceitful, he decided to present himself as someone he was not. That was not on me.

He even came to my house crying, pleading his case, and begging for another chance. He even asked if he could speak to my friend Chris, as if that was going to change my mind. I also have to admit that when he sat in front of me crying, saying that he couldn't lose me and he would go crazy if he wasn't with me and he wanted us to go to therapy together, I actually felt sorry for him for a minute. Then I snapped out of it and reminded myself that I have to protect my peace. And being with someone whom I can't trust is not protecting my peace in any way. I stuck to my guns, and it was over. It felt so freeing that I was finally able to choose me. I will always protect my peace at all costs. This relationship showed me that I can trust myself, and I was beyond proud of myself.

The last question that my therapist asked me was, "What would your life look like if you were unbothered by the ruthlessness of the world around you?" This one was rather easy for me to answer.

Me being unbothered by the ruthlessness of the world around me would allow me to step out of my comfort zone and do all of the things that are on my bucket list that I have been scared to do. Some of those things are travel to all fifty states, book a solo travel trip, make new friends, write a book, and trust myself enough to put myself out there and find my soul mate. Oftentimes the news scares us from living our best lives. The media will tell you that it is unsafe to travel by yourself. But then I think about the work trips I have been on that have resulted in me traveling by myself, and I was just fine each time. I have also traveled to NYC by myself by train at least three times. And each time I went to NYC by myself, I learned something new about the city.

I also made the decision to write this book. I talked myself out of it more times than I can count by convincing myself that no one would care about my story or people would call me dumb because I chose to be totally transparent and vulnerable in this book. But if I want to live my life on my terms, I have to be unbothered by the negativity of others. If we live our lives constantly worried about what others will say, think, or do, then that is not living at all. So here you are reading my book because I decided to tell my story no matter what anyone thought about it. At the end of the day, me writing this book was so therapeutic for me. Seeing where I came from to where I am now does nothing but make me smile.

Protecting your peace is more about a state of being than doing. Finding your inner peace requires you to be fully present in the moment and focused on the task at hand. Protecting your peace has so many benefits such as self-confidence, positive mental and physical health, better relationships, and an overall blissful life. This concept is so important to me because I know that in order for me to be happy, I have to protect my peace. So how does one work on protecting their peace? Here are a few ways you can accomplish this.

1. Pay attention to your triggers. Do you notice that every time you talk to a certain person, you feel emotionally drained or are in a negative space? Does speaking about certain topics make you sad, angry, or uncomfortable? Does being in certain environments make you feel uneasy? Does watching the news or hanging around a certain person make you feel crazy? If you answer yes to any of these questions, it is imperative to limit your time doing these things or stay away from these people if you can. Sometimes, it is impossible to avoid certain people (i.e., your boss, coworkers, toxic family members), and if that is the case, you have to take control over your thoughts, which I will explain next.

2. Take control over your thoughts. Our thoughts determine our mind state, and as a result, they are directly related to our level of peace, which is why you should always be very careful about what you think and how you think. For example, if you are driving to work and already thinking about how that annoying coworker or micromanaging supervisor is going to get on your nerves today, then you can rest assured that they will do just that. Be more intentional with your thoughts, and make sure that they are positive.

3. Take a break from social media. Every once in a while, I take a much-needed break from social media. Sometimes I can go down the rabbit hole of scrolling through my time line, and I see how happy people are (or at least ap-

pear to be) in their relationship or how they just got a new promotion, new car, etc., and then I find myself comparing my life to theirs, not realizing that anybody can make their life appear to be a certain way online. The old adage is comparison is the thief of joy. You have to run your own race. Not to mention how negativity is constantly being spread on social media as well. It's so important to take a break from social media so that these things don't negatively impact your mental state.

4. Stop caring about what other people think. Seeking external validation is one of the quickest ways to allow other people to control your level of peace. You are accountable for your thoughts and actions.

5. Find positive ways to express negative feelings. Go to the gym, meditate, listen to music, vent to a trusted person, journal.

6. Always have a grateful heart. Just remember there is always something that you should be grateful for. Focus on those things, and watch how your inner peace shifts.

7. Accept what you can't change. The quickest way to disturb your inner peace is to worry about things you cannot change. When situations arise that there is absolutely nothing you can do about them, there's really no point in worrying.

8. Love yourself. Once you accept who you are and love yourself unconditionally, doing so brings an unexplainable level of peace.

The best way to protect your peace is to remove the stress. I challenge you to find at least two things on this list that you will commit to implementing to assist in protecting your peace. Life can get hectic and busy. But despite that, we all have the responsibility to take care of ourselves. You have the right to be tired, you don't have to fix everything that is broken, and you certainly don't have to make everyone happy. Make a commitment to yourself today to protect your peace.

CHAPTER 11

Finally Free

No one outside ourselves can rule us inwardly.
When we know this we become free.
—Buddha

This quote meant so much to me when I read it because it is so true. The day when you accept that you are the only one in charge of your peace, happiness, and overall well-being, that is the day when you are totally free. Some say that they are free, but when you truly experience being free, it is a feeling like no other. I worked hard to get to where I am today: totally free, being unapologetically me, and not giving a damn what anyone thinks about me. I have been freed from the shackles of guilt, shame, defeat, hurt, and, most importantly, not loving myself. I look at myself in the mirror every day and tell myself how beautiful I am.

I spent the end of 2019 with an activity that my therapist gave me. It was a packet that talked about the past year and the year ahead. This was a great way to prepare for the year ahead. I gave a packet to my mom and my friend Zahirah because I felt like we were all at crossroads in our lives. I want to share with you the most helpful activities in hopes that you will take the time to do this for yourself at the end and the beginning of each year. I am not just sharing the activities but my answers to each activity as well. This was such an important and pivotal moment for me because it really helped me see how far I came.

The first page asked me to go through my calendar week by week and write down all of the important events for 2019. After I wrote it down, I felt very accomplished.

In January, I decided to take my health back, and I had weight-loss surgery, and I also had my first paid gig for my business, Change Agents for Organizational Success, LLC, doing a five-hour training on grant writing.

In March, my brother Jamaal and I presented at a National Fatherhood Conference in Los Angeles, and we *killed* it.

In April, my family and I all traveled together out of the country to Jamaica. This was my parents' first time in Jamaica, so I was glad to share in that experience with them. This was also my first trip post-weight-loss surgery, and I think I handled it well.

In July, my parents and my brothers formed our family business, Scott 5 Enterprises, LLC. We pooled all of our expertise together to create a powerhouse of a business, so *stay tuned*.

In August, we went to Alabama for our family vacation. We rented a van and rode together and learned a lot about African American history. I loved seeing my father and my younger brother, Jamaal, in their element. It was so inspiring.

In October, I interviewed for a state position, and I slayed the interview. This was the first time that I spoke so highly of myself and actually believed it. I was ultimately selected as the candidate of choice. More money, more diversity, more opportunities.

In November, my mother and I attended a vision board party. To this day, I look at my vision board every morning. I am truly manifesting my destiny.

And finally, in December, I had an appointment with Dr. Yolanda Ragland, a.k.a. Dr. Fix Your Feet. Anyone that really knows me knows that I have been self-conscious about my feet for over fifteen years. I met with her, and not only did she have an amazing spirit, but I was approved for bilateral reconstruction surgery to take place in February 2020.

I was also able to dig a little deeper with the next exercise. The next exercise was six sentences about my past year.

1. The wisest decision I made...I had weight-loss surgery. It saved my life.
2. The biggest lesson I learned...no external factors can make me feel loved. At the end of the day, I have to love myself. My true happiness comes from within.
3. The biggest risk I took...I put myself back out there to date despite being hurt by my exes. I risked being hurt again, and I was, but I learned to trust myself.
4. The biggest surprise of the year...my younger brother Jamaal and I make a great team, and we took the country by storm and presented multiple times on a very important topic: father engagement.
5. The most important thing I did for others...Jamaal and I presented multiple times across the county to practitioners and fathers about the importance of fathers being involved in their kids' lives.

6. The biggest thing I completed…I completed three chapters of my book.

The next exercise was six questions about my past year.

1. What are you most proud of? Losing over one hundred pounds and becoming healthier. No more high blood pressure or sleep apnea, and I have improved mental health.
2. What were you not able to accomplish? I didn't finish my book.
3. What is the best thing that I have discovered about myself? That I am enough just as I am.
4. What am I most grateful for? The fact that I didn't give up on myself and I chose life over death.
5. Who are the three people that influenced you the most? My mom, my therapist, and my friends.
6. Who are the three people you influenced the most? My family in terms of taking their health seriously, my friends, and my daughter.

My three greatest accomplishments from 2019 are:

1. I lost over one hundred pounds.
2. I started writing a book.
3. I FORGAVE MYSELF.

What have I done to achieve these?

1. Became disciplined, ate better, exercised more, had weight-loss surgery, put myself first
2. Opened up more, allowed myself to be vulnerable
3. Therapy, reading, loving myself more and more each day

Who helped you achieve these successes? How?

1. My mom—always my biggest reality check, supporter, encourager, giver of unconditional love. I mean some people say that they can talk to their mom about everything. But when I say everything, I mean everything with no judgment.
2. True friends who provide me with unconditional love, trust, and support
3. My weight loss surgeon and myself because the surgery was simply a tool; I had to work very hard to achieve the results that I did

Three of my biggest challenges of 2019:

1. Forgiving myself
2. Loving myself
3. My relationship with food

Who or what helped me overcome these challenges?

1. My therapist, me, my family, close friends, and mourning the loss of my relationship with food.

What have I learned about myself while overcoming these challenges?

1. That I am truly deserving of all the love and happiness in the world. I am enough just as I am. No one can love me more than I love myself.

FORGIVENESS

Did anything happen during the past year that still needs to be forgiven? Deeds or words that made you feel bad? Or are you angry with yourself? Write it down here. Do good for yourself and forgive. Here is what I wrote here:

> *I allowed Hassan to still manipulate me and use me despite what he did far after our breakup. I still did not love myself enough to cut him completely off. To tell him no. He only talked to me because he needed me. When he got arrested, I still called and checked on him from time to time and even referred him to my lawyer. I was angry with myself but not anymore. I am leaving him in the past. I am free from him.*
>
> *I ask for forgiveness for not being a good friend. For taking the word of a no-good man over my real friends. This was a very costly lesson. But I cannot beat myself up over this anymore. I apologized to my friends for not trusting them. I need to forgive myself for not loving myself. For not having a high sense of self-worth. For speaking so negatively of myself. For not using kind words to myself. I am angry with myself for knowing Rob was lying to me about almost everything and not confronting him sooner. For allowing my fear of being alone to be bigger than my self-worth and self-love. Nicole, I forgive you.*

LETTING GO

Is there anything else I need to say? Is there anything I must let go of before I can start my next year? Draw or write, then think about it, and let it all go:

> *I let go of comparison. I let go of feeling like a failure because I am not married and I have no biological*

102

children. I let go of being disappointed that I didn't make my surgeon's goal weight. I need to let go of the false narrative over my life and my self-limiting beliefs. I need to let go of the external validation from others.

I was so proud of myself when I looked back on the year I had and how much I had grown. It made me that much more optimistic when it came to planning for the year ahead.

The Year Ahead—2020
Dare to Dream Big
What does the year ahead of you look like? What will happen in an ideal case? Why will it be great?

> *I will have completed my book, and I will have an over-whelming sense of accomplishment. I will list my book on Amazon. I will have fully accepted and embraced who I am. I will love myself, I will value myself, and I will exude confidence everywhere I go. I will have paid off the rest of my credit card debt. I will have left the college, and I will travel the country presenting my research and speaking about my book. I will put myself back out there to date with intention.*

MAGICAL TRIPLETS FOR THE YEAR AHEAD

These three things I will love about myself:
1. My sense of humor
2. My body (curves, imperfections, feet)
3. My ability to love unconditionally

I am ready to let go of these three things:
1. My negative self-talk
2. Being so hard and overly critical of myself
3. My need for external validation

These three things I want to achieve the most:
1. Finishing my book
2. Fully loving myself
3. Getting out of debt

These three things I will dare to discover:
1. If I really want to have a child at this age
2. If I can stop being safe, step out on faith, and build my business
3. If my soulmate finds me will I be ready for him

These three things I will have the power to say no to:
1. Inconsistent men
2. Things I don't want to do but feel guilted into doing
3. People trying to take advantage of me

These three things I will do every morning:
1. Wake up with a grateful heart and pray
2. Say my positive affirmations aloud
3. Look at my vision board, and manifest my destiny

I will connect with my loved ones in these three ways:
1. Spending quality time together—vacations, holidays, birthdays, etc.
2. Happy hours
3. Talking more on the phone

With these presents will I reward my success:

1. A new wardrobe (to celebrate reaching my goal weight)
2. A new car
3. A piece of jewelry

SIX SENTENCES ABOUT MY NEXT YEAR

This year I will not procrastinate anymore on…
Finishing my book. I want to be an inspiration to others through this memoir, but I can't if I don't finish. I will not procrastinate anymore on being totally open and vulnerable. This will be the ultimate test of being set free from my past.

This year I will draw the most energy from…
Myself. Everything I need is already within me. I will trust myself. I will love myself. I will be kind to myself.

This year I will be the bravest when…
I know that a man is not right for me and I end it right then and there versus prolonging things when I know I deserve more.

This year I will say yes when…
I am presented with something that will bring me joy. I will say yes when it causes me to step out of my comfort zone. I will say yes when I am scared but I know ultimately saying yes will bring me something great. I will say yes when my spirit moves me positively.

This year I advise myself to…
Go with the flow and not overthink or try to create the narrative of how I think things should be. I will not try to force things that

simply aren't meant to be. I advise myself to let things be just as they are. I advise myself to live in the moment.

This year will be special for me because…
It will be all about me. I finally will choose me over all others. I will be selfish this year. I will put me first in all that I do.

———————

This activity was so important to me for so many reasons. It was the start of a new decade. I was turning forty, and I was finally in the best place mentally, emotionally, and physically. I knew I had to do something very special for my fortieth birthday, so I decided to do something that I have never done for myself in my thirty-nine years on this earth, and that was celebrate myself. I decided to have a fortieth birthday party. I have never had a birthday party in my adult life. Although this was scary for me, I was also looking forward to it. I questioned myself several times during the planning process, saying things like, "What if no one shows up? What if people don't have a good time?" I realized that this was nothing but negative self-talk creeping in, and I would immediately redirect myself.

The day of my party did not start off great at all. I had quite a day with my hair. Another moment of transparency, because in the end, I am finally free, so I am willing to share this part of me too. I suffer from alopecia, and with the weight-loss surgery, it got worse. When my hair started falling out from one of the side effects of surgery, I knew that it would never grow back. But I learned to embrace this about myself, and I started listening to the song "I Am Not My Hair" by India.Arie, and I felt empowered. Me losing my hair doesn't change who I am at the core. Me losing my hair doesn't change the contents of my spirit, my soul, my integrity, and my heart.

My hairstylist, a.k.a. my big sister Nikki, and I decided that we would try something new for my fortieth birthday party. I do not know why I thought that this day would be the day that I totally wanted to switch things up. It ended up being the dumbest decision. I remember cutting the weave out in her bathroom and crying. I called my mom, and she made me feel better, as usual. She soothed my soul and reminded me that everything would be OK. She reminded me that everyone was coming to celebrate me that night. She stayed on the phone with me as she told me to take some deep breaths with her. I did, and I started feeling better. She told me to just go with what I am used to in regard to my hair, and that was what I did. I instantly felt better and started laughing at myself because I was trying to be something different instead of just being me and doing what I was used to.

The end result of my hair was amazing. By this time, I was super late, and I had to rush home so that I could get my makeup done. This was another first for me. In my forty years of life, I had never had my makeup professionally done, so I was super excited about that as well. All I know is she absolutely outdid herself. When I looked at the finished product, I was beyond *amazed*. I looked in the mirror and said to myself, "You are one gorgeous woman." I got dressed and got myself ready to go to my party.

I was so beyond late to my own party. At least an hour late. But I was ready to do my entrance. I picked the song "Lovin' Me" by the R&B Divas. The hook of the song says, "I found me a place where I ain't doing nothing but loving myself and everything about me. I found me a place, and it don't even matter what nobody else thinks because I'm loving me." This truly embodied everything I worked so hard for. Now that you have read my book, I think it is safe to say you can truly understand why I picked this song and why it is so near and dear to my heart. I have truly found a place where I am loving myself and everything about me. I honestly don't care what anyone else thinks because I no longer seek external validation. I embrace myself, flaws and all.

But let me tell you when I walked through those doors, it took everything in me not to fall to my knees and cry. I was overcome with emotion when I looked at all the beautiful faces in that room. From college teammates that I haven't seen in years but every time we get together it's like we never missed a beat (Florida State Seminoles for life), to friends who flew into town to celebrate me, from coworkers new and old who have now become family, to my biological family and my daughter—my God, seeing my daughter the happiest she had been in years—to my friends who have been there through thick and thin. It was such an unexplainable feeling.

It was at that moment that it clicked for me. My life was already full of love. I do not need a man or a relationship to provide that to me. My heart is full. I am not alone. My life is rich. We danced the night away, and I had the time of my life that night. The energy was great from everyone in attendance. We laughed, we reminisced and most of all we loved on each other. I will never forget this day ever because it was truly the night that I was FINALLY FREE!

I can say that so far 2020 has been the Year of Yes. This year of being FORTY, FINE, AND FABULOUS so far owes me nothing, I have done nothing but live truly for me. I got surgery the next month to fix my feet. I allowed myself to be taken care of during this time that I was incapacitated. My dad was so good to me during this time. I honestly believe that this surgery allowed us to bond more. I truly felt like his baby girl. I have been more social and started to go out more. I have some pretty amazing friends. My relationship with my brothers has gotten stronger. My mom and I have always had a solid relationship, but seeing 2020 bring her some amazing blessings makes my heart so full.

I also met an amazing man that showed me that when a man is truly interested in you, he will pursue you. Manny and I had met a little before I had surgery on my feet. We talked every day before my surgery, but we never met up. He knew that I was stressing at my job trying to prepare to go out on medical leave, so he offered to bring me lunch many times. However, we never connected. We would talk on the phone for hours and text each other all day.

I still really didn't think much of it at the time because I wasn't clear of his intentions at first. Something that was beyond refreshing about him was that he was transparent from the start. He told me the good, the bad, and the ugly about himself. I didn't have to poke or pry, I didn't have to turn into a supersleuth—he just told me. And although some of the things he told me were overwhelming, I appreciated his honesty from day one, which gave me the opportunity to decide for myself if I wanted to continue getting to know him. He was so complimentary calling me pretty, beautiful, or making up other unique names for me that would always make me smile. Unbeknownst to him, words of affirmation is one of my love languages, so he was really making my heart melt.

But what really made me see him differently was when he took me out on a date after I had surgery. I mean he took me out on a date with my feet completely bandaged, in my postoperative shoes (which were absolutely hideous, by the way), and lounge clothes. I met him for the first time in yoga pants, a T-shirt, and a hoodie. I was so self-conscious that day because anyone that knows me knows that I love to get dressed up. But he made me feel like I was the most beautiful woman in the world that day. He told me how beautiful I was and didn't mind one bit that I was not at my best. We went to the movies to see *The Photograph* with Issa Rae. We grabbed lunch afterward, and because I was staying at my parents' house during my recovery, he even offered to drive me all the way home to my house to pick up a few things that I needed. I felt so bad that he was literally driving me around all day, so I offered him gas money. He refused the money and told me that it was refreshing to meet someone like me who was not all about what I could get out of a man.

What I really like about him is he is very passionate, affectionate, and complimentary and has a sense of humor that is just as, if not more, inappropriate than mine. The crazy thing about this is that two weeks after our first date he left to go to Michigan on assignment for work, and he would be gone for three months. I initially thought that this was a sign that we were just not meant to be. I just knew that this was going to be the end of us getting to know each other because how could we possibly make it when we were so new? However, he shocked me. We literally talked damn near his whole drive up there (which was eight hours). Not to mention he drove back home to see me after being away for two weeks. He literally worked a ten-hour shift and got right on the road and drove eight hours straight to my house. Now that is consistency.

Although I don't know what is going to happen between Manny and me, all I know is that we will be friends for life. He said to me, "When I say I got you, I got you," and he has held true to that so far. He has quickly become my best friend whom I talk to about everything, and I truly value his advice. I know that he has my best interest at heart, and that is so refreshing.

And on top of that he showed me that a man can be open, vulnerable, consistent, affectionate, and truthful. He is the one to show me that all men are not the same. For that, I will always be grateful for God bringing Manny into my life. I will enjoy the ride for now and see where things take us. Hopefully it is something great that I have hoped for all of my life, which is true love and a soul mate. Either way, I will have a friend for life.

I am truly excited for not just this year but for the many years to come. I want to leave you with some encouragement. Please know that even though you may be going through a dark storm right now, just getting through one, or you can feel one brewing right now, it is not the end. Our pain has a purpose, and for everything we go through in life, there is a reason behind it. Whether it is so that your test and trials can be used as a vehicle to inspire others, whether it's for you to recognize your own strength, or whether it's for you to take time out to face the facts so that you can find a deeper understanding of who you are, all I can say is trust the process. I encourage you to own your darkest moments because there will be something amazing on the other side. I am a living testimony that even if you had some bad chapters in your life, your story can still end well. I am finally free!